Vile Jelly

VILE JELLY

The Birth, Life, and Lingering Death
of
the Arts Council of Great Britain

by

John Pick

Brynmill

first published 1991 by
The Brynmill Press Ltd,
Cross Hill Cottage, Gringley-on-the-Hill,
by Doncaster, S. Yorks. DN10 4RE England

typeset by the Publishers and printed in England

I.S.B.N. 0 907839 52 5

Contents

Dedication and Thanks

To those, mercifully numerous, people
who have talked (or argued) with me
about the Arts Council,
and who have, by their writing, helped me
think about the subject

To Dr Denis Donegan, who can match all British horror stories with American ones, and who has explored with me some of the more cob-webby corners of the shaky old building, to Dr Eric Moody and to Dr Michael Hammet, who in their different ways and at different times have been ready with food for thought and who are always on the lookout for bureaucratic ironies, to Dr Malcolm Anderton, whose researcher's mind and eye for detail during our explorations has often stopped me making a complete fool of myself, Ian Watson, who makes me laugh almost as much as the Arts Council's Annual Report nowadays does (though he means to). And to Dr Caroline Gardiner, John Elsom, Peter Stark, Keith Diggle, Vivian Nixson, Sir Roy Shaw, Professor David Throsby, Jenny Pennington, Robert Hutchison, Professor Anthony Field, Sir Kingsley Amis, Peter Hepple, Dr Alan Tomkins and those many others who have spurred me by their spoken or written insights into state bureaucracy and state subsidy systems. Most particularly my thanks are due to Ian Robinson.

J. P.

Introduction

It is not unreasonable to ask why there should be yet another book about the Arts Council of Great Britain. Quite apart from the Council's own annual reports, occasional pamphlets, strategies, policy papers and other *apologia*, there have already been thirty or more books since the war describing the Council's doings. Some, including I. Evans & M. Glasgow, *The Arts in Britain* (1949), E. White, *The Arts Council of Great Britain* (1965), J. S. Harris, *Government Patronage of the Arts in Great Britain* (1970), and H. Baldry, *The Case for the Arts* (1981) have been broadly appreciative of the Council. Others, such as R. Hutchison, *The Politics of the Arts Council* (1984), B. Appleyard, *The Culture Club* (1984) and my own *Managing the Arts? The British Experience* (1986) have been more critical.

That sequence of dates is suggestive of a shift in attitude. And indeed most comment on the Council in books, journals and newspapers seemed to stop being respectful and restrained somewhere in the mid-seventies. Thereafter there was a good deal of hostility—from the left in the T.U.C. Working Party *Report on the Arts* (1976) and S. Braden, *Artists and People* (1978), from the right in the Selsdon Group's *A Policy for the Arts: Just Cut Taxes* (1977) and Kingsley Amis, *An Arts Policy?* (1979), and from the centre in a pamphlet written for the Liberal Party, J. Elsom, *The Arts—Change and Choice* (1978).

By the time Professor Baldry's book appeared, therefore, there was already some disquiet, even within the London intelligentsia, about the Arts Council, and some quite savage criticism of its adopted methods. Critics of the Council took different points of view—which the Council's defenders took as a bonus, arguing that attacks from opposite viewpoints cancelled themselves out—but as the Council made a virtue of its pragmatism ("Our policy is to have no policy") it could scarcely take comfort from its critics' similar lack of unified principle.

Certainly the publication of Baldry's *Case for the Arts* did more to embolden the critics than confound them. Although the book presented itself as a *case* for state aid in general and the Arts Council in particular, it asserted, rather than argued for, a series of dubious axioms about "policy", "funding" and "the arts". There was the strange assumption that the arts in Britain were essentially those things in receipt of subsidy from the Arts Council (one passage in the book describes the Council solemnly

discussing whether Jazz was deserving of state subsidy, and therefore
worthy of elevation to the status of an art). A second assumption was
odder still. The author seemed to believe that a lively system for dispens-
ing state aid was more or less the same thing as having a lively arts scene.
As Sir Kingsley Amis later remarked:

> The Arts Council and its beneficiaries have wrong-footed the
> opposition to them by dividing the world into good chaps who like
> the arts and so naturally want as much money as possible spent on
> them, and bad chaps who hate the arts and want to starve them or
> even close them down. So of course a book called *The Case for the
> Arts* turns out to put the case for the public subsidy of them,
> whereas a book with that title ought to be putting the contrary
> view.[1]

The Case for the Arts described the functioning of the Arts Council's
panels, its relationship to government and "the arm's length principle"
in painstaking detail, as if a refusal by any reasonable person to pledge
eternal allegiance to each part of the system could only spring from a
failure to understand it properly. Yet two years previously, Hugh Jenkins
had, in *The Culture Gap* (1979), shown that it was possible to like the arts,
to be reasonable, to be politically mature—indeed to be Minister for the
Arts—and still neither believe in the way the Arts Council constituted
itself, nor in the sacredness of a "principle" which seemed to suggest that
the elected politicians were *by their nature* less suited to making decisions
about the arts than were civil servants, or the amateur politicians and
industrialists who sat on the national Arts Council.

Nor did the Council want for attention from other sources. Successive
governments added to the arts reviews in the annual H.M.S.O. *Life in
Britain* publications a series of special reports: *Government and the Arts in
Britain* (1958), *Government and the Arts 1958–64* (1964), the White Paper *A
Policy for the Arts* (1965), *Report on the Arts* (1974) and *The Promotion of the
Arts in Britain* (1975). The Education, Science and Arts Committee of the
House of Commons produced its own voluminous report *Public and
Private Funding of the Arts* in 1982, and each of the main political parties
produced extensive "arts policy" documents at each election. These
usually, but not invariably, proposed radical alterations in the state aiding
system, but ignored the condition of art and artists. Cultural historians
naturally turned their attention to the Council; its conception and birth
are fully described in J. Minihan, *The Nationalisation of Culture* (1977), and
it occupies a significant role in R. Hewison, *In Anger: Culture in the Cold
War* (1981). Economists and sociologists have attempted to unravel its
mysteries, the former exemplified by M. Blaug, *The Economics of the Arts*

(1970), the latter by S. Parker and J. T. Howarth, *Leisure and Public Policy* (1975). Independent foundations commissioned other reports. Among the significant Gulbenkian publications are Lord Bridges, *Help for the Arts* (1959) and Lord Redcliffe-Maud, *Support for the Arts in England and Wales* (1976).

These publications—which represent no more than a fraction of what has been written by and about the Arts Council—contain in total more than 3,000 pages. But this modest *oeuvre* by no means satisfies the relentless craving among arts officials for their bureaucratic system to be described, examined, stripped to its constituent parts, and reassembled yearly, monthly, *daily*, by means of special conferences, enquiries, assessments, surveys and other official stratagems. The narcissistic craving for self-examination is one of the distinguishing characteristics of the modern arts bureaucrat, and thus of Arts Council officers. Each report produces its counter-report. Some reports simply call for more reports. Some constructs within the arts—the four London orchestras for example—seem to have been assembled specifically to provide a topic for reports. It is a barren week, in the high report season, when two or three arts reports do not slither from the duplicating machines.

So it was, in December 1988, in a year which had already seen the publication of some half a dozen books on state funding and "arts policy", most of which contained in their turn references to the hundreds of pamphlets, reports, books, position papers and strategic documents concerned with the state arts system during the eighties, that the Arts Minister Richard Luce wrote to the Chairman of the Arts Council:

> It is appropriate and timely to consider whether the existing arrangements and structure for the support and funding of the arts through the Arts Council and the Regional Arts Associations can be improved. All such systems need scrutiny from time to time to check whether they are still the best that can be devised. The Arts Council has recently carried out an internal management review, and some Regional Arts Associations are revising their structures and practices. So far, however, there has been no review of the system as a whole to see how its constituent parts, with any changes they are planning, can best fit together....

This led to a 91-page report, prepared by the retiring Head of the Government's Office of Arts and Libraries (the office which has administered Britain's direct state aid to its museums, galleries and libraries, and which has annually passed on a smaller sum as the government grant to the Arts Council). This was R. Wilding, *Supporting the Arts: a Review of the Structure of Arts Funding* (1989). Although in its turn it led to the customary showers of meetings, conferences, papers, pamphlets, news-paper articles and reports in all the customary Arts Council-related places, there was a feeling that this time a watershed had been reached. In anticipation of its publication the Secretary General of the Arts Council had written in the Annual Report (1988–9):

> We shall welcome any changes that lead to a better deal for the arts. We shall not welcome change for change's sake. We shall defend to the hilt [sic] that which has been built up over 40 years of funding by an institution, the Arts Council, operating entirely at arm's length from the governments that have funded it.

But the Arts Council was stabbed by those nearest to it, and with whom it had sought to ingratiate itself—et tu Luce—and its sword had been handed to a new chairman who had no inclination to defend the old ways. The Minister announced that the Arts Council's role as a funding agency was to be severely curtailed, and its staff cut. He was congratu-lated on all sides of the House of Commons. A House of Lords debate (though solemnly addressed, with many dire warnings as to what the loss of the Arts Council could mean for civilization, by Lords Goodman and Rees-Mogg) did nothing to dispel the feeling that the Arts Council was on its last legs. Throughout the nation arts bureaucrats reached for their word-processors, and began jockeying for positions in the new bureau-cratic order. Soon new strategies and reports began to appear, and we seemed to be in for a veritable avalanche of words, telling us what bureaucratic life was going to be like after Luce's mortal thrust.

Why then add to it all? When so much has already been written, and when so many interested parties are busying themselves in writing more, why produce yet another description of the Arts Council's lifetime? To which the short answer is that the Council now places its own survival above its duty to the arts. It has become a detached political entity, serving neither artists nor society. In the words of Lord Rees-Mogg it has become "the government's arm" for dealing with the arts. Thus, given its willingness to sail under any flag of covenience, the political storm which Richard Luce's decision set going could even yet, paradoxically, be the saving of it. A series of distracting questions—what is to replace it? how can we keep our national flagship companies afloat without it? what other prestigious mooring could be found for businessmen on the make if there is no Arts Council?—will leave us confused, and we shall feel that the Arts Council had its uses after all.

For Luce had made it clear that the Council would retain "responsi-bility" for the "flagship companies"—the Royal National Theatre, the Royal Opera House, the Royal Shakespeare Company and the English

National Opera. And when it was announced that the shrinking Council (which once had 1,200 clients) would still retain control for the time being of some seventy-seven others, Arts Council officers adopted a somewhat unbecoming defiance. The patient would pull through after all! The latest Secretary General announced that the Council would retain a firmer grasp on managerial matters than had been expected. So, given its oft-repeated assertion that what is good for the Arts Council is good for the arts—given, that is, its obvious desire at all costs to preserve itself—can we really expect it to do its duty, carry its lighter cargo until that in turn is off-loaded into another vessel, and then sink gently from view? From all we know of it, is it not more likely that it will trim its sails, wait for a new political wind, and make for the new harbour? Then, when it is safely berthed, and a sympathetic Minister appointed—Luce had two successors in 1990—there will follow the announcement that it has once more set up an enquiry into itself, that new code words have been suggested for the nineties, and that events have shown, after all, that it has a new and indispensable strategic role.

The further harm that would do can hardly be imagined. The central objection to the Arts Council is that it has created an arts bureaucracy which makes its claim upon our attention by its political, managerial and marketing know-how, rather than by its ability to be alert to good art and by the quality of its critical judgements. It has thus betrayed the best hopes of its founders. A part of that betrayal has been the persistent misuse of critical language. (The Council's notion of "excellence" in an arts organization, for example, involving as it does notions of the organization's economics, management, and scale of operation, is quite different from what a real critic means by excellence.) Another part has been the persistent application to the arts of terms which properly belong to other realms—"efficiency", "optimum output", "key managerial aims".

Further, the Council has chosen to make a virtue of having no consistent, or coherent, principles, but has claimed instead that its own organizational structure and status *ensure* that its judgements will be disinterested and good. Palpably this is untrue. When the Council makes good judgements—as on occasions it has, of course—it has made them because of the excellence of the people working for it, not because of qualities somehow embedded within its managerial frame. The "arm's length principle", and "peer group assessment" are not in themselves any kind of guarantee that good decisions will be taken. Moreover they are no defence against Arts Council officers being, individually or collectively, small-minded, crass and wrong.

And that is what, most particularly in the eighties, so many of the

Council's officers have been. The gleeful adoption of the language of the enterprise economy, the replacement of any pretence at critical judgement in the arts by a half-baked form of management "assessment" of arts organization, and the craven desire to please government by adopting its most tendentious economic notions (about "reviving the inner cities", for example) as if they were received truths, together mean that the Council has, more or less completely, destroyed its credibility with artists and public. It has shown that it can no longer recognize artistic excellence, nor indeed recognize art; it can operate only within the crass political realm from which it was supposedly defending artists and the arts, and can therefore only recognize and respond to political and managerial symptoms displayed by its remaining clients. One more book, which summarizes the evidence for a final judgement, is therefore needed. Then, in the name of artists, of art, and of good arts criticism, the order must go out, *Sink the Arts Council!*

*   *   *

There is virtue in brevity. Much of this is well-known territory. Each region has been explored, recorded and argued-over in detail. What is now needed—to make the telling point—is that the map be viewed whole, so that the larger lettering can be clearly read.

Then it will be clear that the British Arts Council is now not really an *arts* council at all. It has sought to keep itself alive by using what it terms "the arts" (a strange concoction in many respects, the Arts Council's "arts") as a peg on which to hang its ideas on social engineering, education, urban planning, economics, management, marketing, tourism, wealth-creation, enterprise and politics. And, when it is really up against it, it always returns to what John Maynard Keynes called the Arts Council's "biggest problem"—putting up state arts buildings. In times of stress it becomes a builder's merchant or, to use a spivvish old word in its newly honourable sense, it moves into *development*.

Its ideas about all these things—social engineering, education, urban planning and so on—are nearly always mundane, and always second-hand. But even if they *were* any good—even if, say, the Council had really thought carefully about what "tourism" does to the relationship between artist and audience, and not just parroted government propaganda about "tourism's" supposed economic value—the Arts Council would still have betrayed the arts. Because when we make economic, political or managerial judgements that are intermingled with artistic judgements—as the Arts Council has for the last fifteen years and more determinedly intermingled them—the result is *inevitably* a distortion, an *artistic* misjudgement. Artistic quality is not, as so many Arts Council

officers have said, *one* of the things that needs to be taken into considera-
tion when coming to a judgement, it is *everything*.

Those who have worked for the Arts Council, and its remaining well-
wishers who believe there is yet some hope that it can be revived, will of
course say that there were times (in its earlier years) when the Council
knew full well that critical alertness was everything, and knew that the
Council could only justify its existence if it appointed people able to stand
firm on their own good judgement. There was also a time when—as its
part of the arm's length principle—the Arts Council left politics to the
politicians, social engineering to social workers and education to parents
and teachers. Its defenders may also point out—reasonably enough—that
for long periods in its history the Arts Council recognized that it did not
speak for the entirety of the arts, but for a particular segment of them. All
that may be granted. Yet there comes a point when a body so persistently
acts, speaks, and therefore thinks basely, that it is beyond redemption.
And it is hard to see how an organization which has so far forgotten its
purposes as to say that it intends to promulgate the "enterprise culture",
intends to commit itself as a priority to something called "urban
redevelopment", and which has become so crassly mercantile that it
describes the arts as "a successful part of Great Britain Plc", could ever
function again as an *arts* council.

The Arts Council has, most particularly in the last twenty years,
yielded all of its ground to the values of commerce. It has chosen to
present the commercial world's methods and values as the "real world",
which "the arts" must be taught to live in. Yet if the Arts Council does
not itself believe that it is the arts which are the real world, and does not
believe that it exists to illuminate other realms by the eternal wonder and
delight of art, then it is no arts council. And indeed, it has hardly
bothered to pretend, in recent years, that it *is* a real arts council any more.
Its reports (like those, equally depressing, that now come from our
Universities and Cathedrals) resemble the annual reports of business. The
value that the Council claims to give the government for taxpayers'
money is a purely *economic* value. It is interested in managing, marketing
and making money, all for their own sakes, not for the sake of art.

Here is a report, recently written, about a neo-governmental scheme
for state aiding worthy arts organizations:

> In the first 12 months of the Incentive Funding scheme, almost
> £4·5m was allocated in awards. Those who received awards project
> a total increase of more than £13m in their *annual* self-generated
> income by the end of 1991. Forty-eight arts groups from all over
> Britain have been successful in their bids for incentive funds. Suc-
> cessful applications are based on sound three-year plans—some-

thing which all organizations should have readily available—and on
plans which should be of real benefit to organizations whether or
not they receive an award. This year we have simplified both the
guidelines and the application process, to rebut any lingering criticism that the scheme is unnecessarily complex and bureaucratic.
And the Council has approved an extension to the scheme which is
designed to provide training and other help to arts organisations at
an early state in the planning process.

An incentive scheme is a stimulus for private sector contribution
to the arts, and the scheme as a whole is an agent for encouraging
the arts world towards better management practice and greater
self-reliance. More and more arts groups are testifying to the
scheme's success.

It obviously does not strike the author as incongruous that taxpayers'
money should be used to give state bribes to people to cadge from the
private sector, nor does he see that it may be premature, after only twelve
months' experience of the new scheme, to describe any criticism as
"lingering". We are obviously meant to take on trust the news that,
down the long months of its operation, "more and more" arts groups are
testifying ("testifying"—where do they testify?) to its "success". Obviously, this is written by a child of the eighties, by someone whose time-
span is linked to the flashing of a stock-exchange computer screen,
someone who believes excellence to be marked solely by managerial
expertise and the accumulation of wealth. It is obviously someone with
little interest in the slow and unpredictable processes of artistic creation,
or in the gradual and unplannable evolution of real artistic talent. This, in
another decade, might have been thought odd, as the author was at the
time Secretary General of the Arts Council of Great Britain, giving an
account of his stewardship in the Arts Council Annual Report 1988–9.
(The Report is reprinted in Appendix A.)

Yet nowadays it is not thought odd. The Arts Council no longer sees
itself as a ship of state, but as king of the realm, the "flagship companies" metamorphosed into jewels in its crown. And in its fading years
this king has taken to wearing garments and ornaments which at first
seemed odd, but which have now cleaved to the body "with the aid of
use". The educational cloak with which Keynes first hid the infant's
artistic nakedness was in the sixties covered by its golden sociological
one. Then in middle age it took to carrying the sceptre of economics, set
off by the doublet of cultural enterprise topped with the developer's
hood. Now, with the chains of urban redevelopment about its shoulders,
and clutching the sceptre of devolution, this old body stares at us
defiantly, determined in the face of all opposition to live through its dark

night and to conquer new kingdoms, but:

> 'Tis not the balm, the sceptre and the ball,
> The sword, the mace, the crown imperial,
> The intertissued robe of gold and pearl,
> The sacred title running 'fore the king,
> The throne he sits on, nor the tide of pomp,
> That beats upon the high shore of this world,
> No, not all these, thrice-gorgeous ceremony,
> Not all these, laid in bed majestical,
> Can sleep so soundly as the wretched slave,
> Who with a body fill'd and vacant mind
> Gets him to rest, cramm'd with distressful bread;
> Never sees horrid night, the child of hell,
> But, like a lackey, from the rise to set,
> Sweats in the eye of Phoebus, and all night
> Sleeps in Elysium.

The early Arts Council was, wilfully, confused about its aims and purposes, and it hid its dark ambitions to make state art compulsory—but in the event it generally acted as a reactive and modest body. In middle age its desire to plan and to control took over, and it became tetchy, believing itself uniquely possessed of the power to bestow the titles of art and excellence by bureaucratic edict. In old age, lonely and demented, it tried to *use* art to achieve the economic and political ends to which it had been converted, and in its dementia it began to call its own bureaucratic processes "the arts". The only end there can be to this sad progression now described in its seven ages, is to allow the Council the dignity of eternal sleep.

1
Brought to Birth

Lord Keynes announced in a broadcast in July 1945 that Britain had an Arts Council. "It has happened in a very English, informal, unostentatious way—half baked if you like."[1] The "semi-independent" Council was to be "a permanent body, independent in constitution, free from red tape, but financed by the Treasury and ultimately responsible to Parliament".

It was an offspring of C.E.M.A.[2] The wartime experience of that body gave the new Council a substantial inheritance of managerial wisdom:

> At the start our aim was to replace what war had taken away; but we soon found that we were providing what had never existed even in peace time.

And C.E.M.A. bequeathed a considerable authority also. In that same broadcast, within a few hours of the Council's birth, Keynes was able to speak confidently of "We of the Arts Council", and to present an ambitious programme of cultural reform:

> We of the Arts Council are greatly concerned to decentralize and disperse the dramatic and musical and artistic life of the country, to build up provincial centres and to promote corporate life in these matters in every town and county.

He assumed for it an established and indispensable role as mediator between artist and public, and claimed for it a remarkable omniscience in matters of art, criticism and creativity:

> The task of an official body is not to teach or to censor but to give courage, confidence and opportunity. Artists depend on the world they live in and the spirit of the age. There is no reason to suppose that less native genius is born into the world in the ages empty of achievement than in those brief periods when nearly all we most value has been brought to birth. New work will spring up more abundantly in unexpected quarters and in unforeseen shapes when there is a universal opportunity for contact with traditional and contemporary arts in their noblest forms.

In that first broadcast we have before us, ready-formed, many of the now familiar criss-crossing Arts Council themes. From the very beginning there was the assurance that the Council—from its birth to its dotage essentially a product of the metropolis—simultaneously believed in the maintenance of London's "excellence" and in the "devolution" of that same commodity. The devolution at first was to be to somewhere called "the provinces", but, as successive Arts Council officers recycled Keynes's dogmas into the later cants of their times, the provinces became "the regions", and when that in its turn became unconvincing, the geographical notion became a purely economic construct, and activities outside London were wanly described as "regional developments". (All that was in the future: Keynes's own thoughts on the provinces amounted only to a limp chirrup, "Let every part of Merry England be merry in its own way."³)

Here too is the first appearance of the central Arts Council dilemma, the simultaneous desire to respond to "the best", wherever it may occur, and to prescribe for "the most". From its birth to its lingering death the Arts Council of Great Britain blithely put into practice a series of irreconcilable policies. State aiding only the best in art means that there will be unequal distribution of excellence, and access to it, between different parts of the country, and between classes, and every sort of group. A determination on the other hand to distribute Arts Council "excellence" equally around the kingdom, and to give all people equal access to it, means that inevitably you will be state-aiding the second and third best, and supporting organizations more concerned with social manipulation than with art.

We also see here the shadowy first appearance of the archetypal Arts Council bureaucrat, selflessly standing aside from interference with the artist's work, concerned only to assist him in that "real world" of politics and finance in which the artist cannot find his way. ("He cannot be told his direction," Keynes announced authoritatively, "he does not know it himself.") Here too are the first stirrings of a belief that artists must always depend upon politicians, industrialists, economists and the like in the *real world*, without whom they would have no existence, could not be "brought to birth" at all. For that, surely, is the only wisp of meaning that may be drawn from the pronouncement that "Artists depend upon the world they live in and the spirit of the age." Unlike politicians, industrialists and economists, the acknowledged legislators of mankind, artists are dependent upon the constraints of "the world they live in".

Help was, however, at hand. The new Arts Council was there, to give the artist "courage, confidence and opportunity", though not at the request of British artists, nor indeed at the request of the British electorate. Keynes fashioned the Arts Council according to beliefs which either belonged to the salons of Bloomsbury, or were drawn, rather oddly, from the very different experiences of our wartime allies. For it seemed that the Council was going to spread courage and confidence in the arts by the economic means adopted by Roosevelt in the U.S. Federal Aid Programme during the thirties—state aid for local arts organizations—and its political manoeuvres were to be based on those adopted by Stalin's "Ministry of Culture" in the U.S.S.R. "I hear," said Keynes coyly, as if this clinched the argument for building civic "arts centres" all over Britain, "that in Russia theatres and concert halls are given a very high priority in building."

In later decades the vast U.S. programme of federal aid for the arts under Roosevelt, which had so impressed Keynes, tended to be forgotten, and we were usually assured that the Americans envied us "the British system". Meanwhile that system's architects, without acknowledging their inspiration, moved ever closer to the Soviet model. Eventually, in the 1980s, when the Council seemed in most respects to be in the pocket of a radical government proclaiming the virtues of free enterprise, it was demanding from its remaining clients development strategies, three-year plans and market forecasts which uncannily mirrored the language and methods of Moscow's Ministry of Culture.

More than anything, however, Keynes's broadcast manifesto strikes one as cultural appeasement, a desire to smooth over great difficulties and to offer a phrase or two of comfort to all parties, so that at all costs this new body could be created. (With so intelligent a man, it must have been deliberately fashioned to be so.) The great questions about this new Arts Council's fitness for its tasks were never put. The critical questions over the respective merits of Britain's different musical and artistic cultures, the question which any responsible Arts Council should have asked about the oral and written cultures, about ownership of the national drama, about poetry and the novel and all that might be understood by our traditions in art, are smoothed away: "How satisfactory it would be if different parts of the country would again walk their several ways as they once did and learn to develop something different from their neighbours and characteristic of themselves...."

Such blandness inevitably slides into deception. He wants to say that his new body will provide "what had never existed even in peace time", so he must pretend that British art did not really amount to anything much until the coming of the state Arts Council (another strand of Keynes's thinking which his Arts Council successors have enthusiastically endorsed). "There never were many theatres in this country," he announces unblushingly, "or any concert-halls or galleries worth count-

ing." Elsewhere he said that he could count the number of museums in
pre-war Britain on one hand. As there were in fact some hundreds of
museums, theatres and concert halls,[4] we must add yet another reason for
admiring him, for it would appear that Keynes achieved all that he did in
spite of being secretly encumbered with an embarrassing superfluity of
fingers.

Although the British Arts Council drew something of its character
from each of its ill-matched foster-parents—state aid seen as social investment was learned from Roosevelt's federal programmes, and the tech-
niques of prescriptive "policy-making" gradually absorbed from
Moscow's Ministry of Culture—the new body was not imposed upon the
public without first swaddling itself in a guaranteed cloak of respectabil-
ity. Keynes wrapped the new baby in the respectable folds of the British
adult education tradition. Whatever is distinctively British about the early
British Arts Council derives from all that is borrowed from the W.E.A.
and the University Extension Class. Keynes asked his listeners not to
think of the Arts Council as a schoolmaster,[5] but that is flummery, the
Housemaster telling the new boy to look on him as a friend. His tone
throughout is that of the teacher, his vision is of the new Council and the
B.B.C. forming a great new educative partnership; "it is a new game we
are teaching you to play."

Lord Keynes's unblinking assumption of authority, his slightly testy
lecturing style, the condescension and occasional larkiness ("The Arts
Council," he announced jovially, "has joined with the Trustees of the
Crystal Palace in the preparation of plans to make that once again a great
People's Palace"[6]) all combine to make his broadcast sound like a head-
master's speech at the beginning of term, blurring the past, offering
cheery words of comfort to nervous newcomers, and a hearty if slightly
unconvincing optimism about the future. The small band of people who
stood behind Keynes at that time—some already in the new Arts Council,
others highly influential upon it—seemed to see themselves in their
different ways as chosen members of the nation's cultural common room,
from which the general public, bull-necked politicians and the artists
themselves must for their own good be kept at arm's length.

*   *   *

The most schoolmasterly figure in that small cultural common room
was undoubtedly W.E. Williams, wartime Director of the Army Bureau
of Current Affairs, and in peacetime secretary of the British Institute of
Adult Education. In January 1943 he had published an article entitled
"Are We Building a New Culture?",[7] in which he described his dream of
a post-war Britain covered with a national grid of Cultural Centres:

Instead of our present dispersal of the Public Library down one street, the art gallery (if any) down another, the Workingmen's Club somewhere else, and so on, let us plan the Civic Centres where men and women may satisfy the whole range of educational and cultural interests between keeping fit and cultural argument. Let us so unify our popular culture that in every considerable town we may have a centre where people may listen to good music, look at painting, study any subject under the sun, join in a debate, enjoy a game of badminton—and get a mug of beer or cocoa before they go home.

Such a vision is marked less by impracticability (consider just how many badminton courts would have to be built in order for the population, "men and women", to be able to indulge their nightly whim for a game), than by its uncanny similarity, in its general ethos and its detail, to the "Houses of Culture" which have been for so long one of the most depressing features of the communist cities of Eastern Europe. There is the same relish for planning, for getting it all under one official roof, and the same air of soggy joylessness. One sees with sudden clarity what the Arts Council's People's Palace, had it ever been built, would probably have been like—Warsaw's unspeakable Palace of Culture, a post-war "gift" from Stalin.

In early 1943 Williams bases his contention that Britain is "building a new culture" on what he says is a new and growing "demand" for the arts and arts education. Like Keynes, however, he grossly distorts what was happening before the birth of the Arts Council, aggrandizing the extent of wartime demand by implying that before the war Britain was a cultural desert. Its vastly impressive libraries, its universities, its city halls, town halls, and its nine thousand village halls, the myriad places where people had met in the thirties, are all summarily dismissed: "Adult education after this war must no longer be content with the Calvinist notion that any old upper room will do for cultural purposes." In future, it's to the People's Palaces! for your nightly badminton, culture and cocoa.

The excellence of some of the B.B.C.'s broadcasting in wartime is apparent enough, and it would be churlish to deny that the activities of C.E.M.A.—though overpraised by about the same proportion as the more earthy activities of E.N.S.A.[8] have been undervalued—showed some remarkable successes. What needs trimming are the exaggerated claims made then (and since) for the "demand" for art and arts education that the B.B.C. and C.E.M.A. supposedly produced in wartime. There is good reason for scepticism *whenever* we are told that state arts bureaucrats have perceived a new demand. British reports have in each successive decade announced "growing demand" for the subsidized arts, usually as audiences significantly begin to shrink. This "demand" has almost invariably been noted by an arts bureaucrat anxious to extend the scale of his or her operations. At times officers of the Arts Council have been able to discern a general demand for subsidized arts after spending only a few hours in a city, and even on occasion they have sniffed it out without talking to any members of the public at all. Once located, this "demand", unlike demand for other things, becomes a "need", which the state has a "duty" to meet. From Williams onwards, Arts Council officers have had the knack of being able to discern growing demands and the needs of others at a radius of fifty miles. There is by contrast a lengthy roster of genuine requests for help which, coming from unfashionable quarters or falling outside the prescribed categories of state art, have received a dusty answer.

The claims about the size of the great new "demand" for the arts in wartime thus seem largely to have been made by the bureaucratic report-writers. It is they who write of the ordinary people's enthusiasm and gratitude for the wartime arts service. Such comments as exist from "ordinary people" within the C.E.M.A. record and the books of reminiscence bear the marks of benign editing. It is the bureaucrats who tell us how much the ranks enjoyed Sybil Thorndyke and Lewis Casson, how all the munition workers wept at the Bach concerto, and how enthusiastically they joined in the discussions organized by the Army Bureau of Current Affairs. Where there is an attempt to quantify this great popular surge, however, the exaggeration is exposed readily enough. For example, Williams estimates that before the war one adult in 240 regularly took part in Adult Education classes, on a voluntary basis. Most wartime classes were compulsory and so it is no surprise that the numbers attending such classes in wartime rose. However, it does not suit Williams's purpose merely to note this fact. It has to be presented as part of a great change in the national character, a foundation for "the new culture" we are apparently building:

> First, there is the phenomenal extension of group-discussion. This method of hammering out knowledge is nothing new; such bodies as the Workers' Educational Association have practised it for forty years. What is new, and notable, is that this example has suddenly been multiplied a thousandfold.

A thousandfold? One does not need to be possessed of all Keynes's fingers to calculate that if one person in 240 already engages in an activity as fully as it may be engaged in, then multiplying the scale of the activity a thousandfold is impossible. If Williams is to be believed then during the

war Britain actually contained more arts students than people.
A glance at the (compulsory) Army adult education syllabus, to say
nothing of a glance at the surviving photographs of sullen and embar-
rassed wartime students, will do something to modify the picture Williams paints of the general cultural euphoria. The "sudden"
multiplication of interest in education (significant, of course, but for other
reasons) was in large measure brought about by order of the authorities,
and the core syllabus comprised basic training in literacy and numeracy,
foreign affairs lectures, simple civics, some crafts and a little economics
and history. The discussions which followed the presentation of ABCA
playlets were of course more wide-ranging, but that was small beer, and
overall "the arts" naturally enough rested on the margins of wartime life.

Williams's 1943 article nevertheless contained a three-point plan for
consolidating the new, notable and sudden demand for artistic excellence,
and for building the exciting new post-war British culture. The plan was:

> 1   A post-war Ministry of Education to organize education for
> adults on a massive scale.
> 2   Civic Centres where men and women can satisfy their educa-
> tional interest.
> 3   A sample plan for the popular arts; painting, music, literature
> etc.

Shorn of hyperbole, it is flabby stuff, and even by later Arts Council
standards, remarkably non-committal. There is no indication, for
example, as to what "a sample plan" for the popular arts might actually
look like. There is no way of knowing what he imagines will be the
"educational interests" of post-war British "men and women", nor of
how Civic Centres may be designed to "satisfy" such an unknowable
demand. In the midst of the fog there can however be heard the voice of
the cultural Tsar: *planning* the popular arts and *organizing* education, so
the two things meld together in nationally-planned *Civic Centres*, all on a
massive scale.

There are many ways in which Williams's article strikes the same
chords as Keynes's later broadcast, but there are times too when his po-
faced promotion of vast cultural schemes is so obviously at odds with the
essentially drawing-room character of Williams's real world, that it all
bellyflops into unintended farce:

> Even bolder in its conceptions and more popular in its appeal is the
> art project in British restaurants, organized by Lady Clark[9] for the
> British Institute of Adult Education. In these strategic spots thou-
> sands of men and women are having, for the first time in their lives,
> the chance to look at the paintings and lithographs and mural

decoration which Lady Clark has collected and displayed for the pleasure and edification of the people of Greater London. It is an example which leads to the hope that the day may come when the art treasures of this country, released from the Chained-Bible stage in which they so often remain today, will be exhibited in those places where the community works and eats and waits for a train.

Anybody who spends much time in places where the community works or eats or waits for a train will probably fear that exhibiting the art treasures of this country in them would be anything but an educational act. And proposing to base a great cultural revolution upon the fact that Lady Clark has hung her lithographs in a place where people may glance at them as they wait for their spam and chips is derisory. But, again, speaking of political gestures, where have we heard of pictures hanging in railway stations, of free short stories distributed at bus stops, of state art compulsorily toured around a nation's workplaces, or dangled before those queueing in works canteens? Where else but the U.S.S.R. once more! The Soviet state planners also call any large assembly of manual workers a "community", and all forward planning in the arts is likewise termed "development". One is bound to observe that many of Williams's pronouncements would have gone through on the nod in the Soviet Ministry of Culture.

*   *   *

A third figure in at the birth of the Arts Council was Sir Kenneth (later Lord) Clark. It would be hard to find a public figure whose pronouncements would, by contrast, have caused more bewilderment within the Soviet Ministry. An intellectual and aesthete, who wrote that he had never, until the sudden collapse of his self-confidence late in life, doubted his artistic judgement even for a single moment, patrician in manner, with a general contempt for politicians and the disturbing habit of crying frequently in public, Clark was also, in the older sense of the word, a British amateur.

He was, however, and for several decades, a man of affairs in the British cultural cabinet (first chairman of I.T.V., long-serving B.B.C. Governor, on more than fifty Boards including that of the Covent Garden Opera, on to which he introduced four members of his own family). At the outbreak of war he was Director of the National Gallery, and was soon involved in the creation of C.E.M.A. In the first year of the war he called on Tom Jones at Coleg Harlech in Wales. Jones was then secretary of the Pilgrim Trust, which had a substantial history of giving grant aid to British arts organizations in the thirties, and Clark intended to ask for the Trust's support of his scheme to employ painters to record aspects of the war:

> I put my plan to him, and after a moment's pause he said, "We are
> already committed to a similar scheme, but I will ask Buck de la
> Warr (then Minister of Education) to see you about it." I went next
> week, and was told that Buck, having already secured a promise of
> £25,000 from the Pilgrim Trust, was going to ask the government
> for a grant of £25,000 to "do something to help the arts". He knew
> what the Treasury answer would be. "We will give you £25,000 if
> you can get an equal sum from other sources." After a decent
> interval he told the Treasury he had raised the necessary money;
> and so there came into existence the body known as the Council for
> the Encouragement of Music and the Arts.

To this body, and later to the Arts Council, Clark brought his absolute
certainty of personal judgement. It is typical of him that he saw no
difficulty for the new body in the recognition of artistic excellence. So
long as they followed his sure and unshakeable critical judgements,
excellence would be acknowledged and artistic knavery vanquished. The
encasement of this process within a respectable managerial framework
presented, by contrast, great political difficulties, though Clark was only
vaguely interested in them: "I remember a good deal of confusion in the
early stages. Who was going to be chairman? The treasury were anxious
to find a place for Lord Macmillan, whose position as Minister of Information was obviously insecure. I believe he remained chairman for three
years...."

When Keynes became chairman of C.E.M.A. in 1942, Clark found
himself on good terms with him, though they never became friends.[10] He
admired Keynes's brilliance, but thought "he displayed it too unspar-
ingly. ... Although a kind man, I have seen him humiliate people in a
cruel way." He saw nothing of the populist streak that is written in to
Keynes's 1945 broadcast, and took a different line from Keynes over
Roosevelt's U.S. federal aid programme:

> The ability to bring off a large mural decoration has been, since
> Tiepolo, extremely rare. ... What finally killed the idea was the
> Federal Arts Scheme in the U.S.A., initiated during the 1930
> depression, and run by conscientious men. It filled public buildings
> with mural paintings, most of which have now been whitewashed
> over. I write this from the old-fashioned point of view that the aim
> of state patronage is to produce good works of art; but I am told
> that at a recent meeting of critics in Oslo it was agreed that the sole
> aim of painting was to support the political system of the state.
> Only the British dissented. Under these circumstances an Arts

Council becomes unnecessary, and its functions can be handed over to a ministry of propaganda.

He saw Keynes as a Cambridge apostle,[11] ruthless in the pursuit of excellence, and contemptuous of the commonplace. If Clark's picture of Keynes is the right one, then Keynes's espousal of populism, of the arts as a social service, in his 1945 broadcast—"Your enjoyment will be our first aim. ...Let every part of England be merry in its own way...a great People's Palace"—was a political trick. It was expedient to pretend that the Arts Council could, somehow, be all things to all men.

* * *

"I do not believe it is yet realized what an important thing has happened. State patronage of the arts has crept in." Keynes thus chose to present the new body as if it were the first time British governments had been involved in subsidizing the arts, and as if an Arts Council of that character were the only possible means by which it might be done. He was of course (as he knew perfectly well) wrong on both counts. From the middle of the eighteenth century, when the British government chose to buy the collection that formed the nucleus of the National Gallery collection, the British government had been almost continuously involved in both direct and indirect financial support of arts organizations, buildings and artists. The Foreign Office had subsidized the performing arts during the First World War, and at the same time, in the way it set up the War Office Cinematograph Board, the government had established the "arm's length principle" that, later, was said by some to have been Keynes's invention. The B.B.C. was similarly established "at arms' length" from government in 1927, and the British Council, another obvious role model for the Arts Council, had been created in 1935. State patronage was in fact long established in Britain.

The Arts Council's emergence from C.E.M.A. in 1945 was moreover achieved only by the sudden brutal despatch of another semi-independent state organization, its much larger counterpart, E.N.S.A. That body had been set up at the outbreak of war, and had operated by rather different means—direct employment of its artists and performers—but it had aims which overlapped with those of C.E.M.A. It was concerned with the popular arts, and with entertainment—Gracie Fields rather than Myra Hess, Noël Coward rather than Elena Gerhardt—but many artists worked for both organizations and they had common ground.

The treasury was however persuaded, by Keynes and others, to continue the work of C.E.M.A. in peacetime (although there is no doubt, as Clark said, that the treasury had previously thought C.E.M.A. would end with the war) and, at the same time, the Whitehall bureaucracy was persuaded to kill off E.N.S.A. Its head, Basil Dean, was not invited, alone of all the wartime chiefs, to take part in the Victory Parade. With E.N.S.A.'s demise went the notion of a state organization acting primarily as direct promoter in the performing arts, so Keynes was able to present the C.E.M.A. method—annual grant aid paid to cover a charitable organizations's deficit—as being the right and proper method to give artists "courage, confidence and opportunity".

Keynes did not mention the sudden despatch of E.N.S.A. in his broadcast. Insidiously, however, in that first broadcast, he took the populist aims of E.N.S.A. and grafted them on to the Arts Council's manifesto. The people's enjoyment had been the first aim of E.N.S.A., but now it became that of C.E.M.A.'s postwar child. E.N.S.A. had existed to promote fine entertainment, and now that too was grafted on to the new Council's aims. "Our war-time experience has led us already to one clear discovery: the unsatisfied demand and the enormous public for serious and fine entertainment." He thus pretends to see no difficulty in saying that general public enjoyment is the Council's first aim, but adding at the same time that the Council exists primarily to maintain and to disperse around the country "the traditional and contemporary arts in their noblest forms".

How did Keynes do it? What was the essential argument that must have clinched it with the civil servants? Why did even the exhausted coalition government give its assent to a body which had no popular support, and, to judge by Keynes's broadcast, only the most tenuous and contradictory notions of how it might function? What persuaded normally parsimonious public servants to give funds to an organization that simultaneously promised the defence of high art and the gratification of the popular will?

There must undoubtedly have been a wish to give Keynes some tangible (and, surely, relatively harmless?) reward for his tireless government work. There must also have been the feeling that "something would have to be done" about the arts during Britain's post-war recovery, and that this was a cheap and simple way of seeming to do it. Yet the evidence from Keynes's broadcast, and from much else, is that the Civil Service was actually expecting the Arts Council to be primarily concerned with the re-opening of the Covent Garden Opera, and with rebuilding theatres and concert halls around the country. It was that which Keynes had stressed. It will, he said, be "our biggest problem", the replacing of all the bombed and derelict theatres, and the building of new concert halls and arts centres where (he said) none had existed before. The Glasgow Citizens' Theatre was "a perfect model of what we should like to see established everywhere."

Everywhere! Plainly the cultural common room had in mind that the new Council's main function outside London would be to erect state arts buildings throughout the land, ten miles from each other, and all exactly the same. Yet it is one of the many paradoxes in this history that in practice the Council had nothing to do with buildings for the first twenty years of its life. What Keynes said was its "biggest problem" was until 1965 unconsidered and remains unsolved. Instead the youthful Council developed a quite different character, and spent much of its time, as youngsters will, considering itself.

2

The Growing Child

So, between its birth and the seminal White Paper of 1965, what did the growing child think that it was doing?

Keynes's manifesto drew together a number of purposes, the chief of which were to:

a) Act as the agency for building, maintaining and restoring theatres, concert halls, galleries and Arts Centres. Providing places, everywhere, for "congregation and enjoyment" was "our biggest problem".

b) Become state patron of the fine arts, and in particular make London "a great artistic metropolis, a place to visit and to wonder at".

c) Be the pump primer. Keynes had often expressed the view that the arts should ultimately be self-supporting. As Harrod[1] recalls, "His ideal for C.E.M.A. was that at the final stage, no doubt not to be reached for a long time, it should have no disbursements, except the cost of administration."

d) Modify the effects of the market economy upon the arts. In Keynes's view the "destruction of the divine gift of the public entertainer by prostituting it to the purposes of financial gain is one of the worser crimes of present-day capitalism. How the state could best play its proper part it is hard to say. We must learn by trial and error. But anything would be better than the present system."[2]

e) Support entertainment and the popular arts. "Your enjoyment will be our first aim."

f) Be a great leveller, to "disperse the dramatic and musical and artistic life of the country", and to build identical arts centres in all inhabited parts of the kingdom.

g) Act as the nation's educator, in partnership with other state agencies, such as the B.B.C.

It is obvious that these purposes are not readily compatible. Indeed they seem, in Raymond Williams's words, to be evidence of "deep-rooted

inconsistencies, incompatible variations; indeed...a radical incoher-
ence."

Williams goes on to suggest of these deep-rooted inconsistencies that it
was nevertheless "evidently possible to hold them all within a single
mind, indeed within a notably clear single mind".[3] The inference Williams expects us to draw from this is clear. Keynes died almost as soon as
the Arts Council was created, but, had he lived (we are to suppose) he
would have made the Arts Council a coherent body, united and pur-
poseful in action, because, secretly, he understood how these apparent
conflicts could be resolved. That indeed is the function of calling
Keynes's mind "notably clear" and "single". Lesser mortals, with their
many minds, reflect in them muddle and confusion which does not exist
within the single-minded man.

Yet the overwhelming evidence is that, although Keynes could "hold"
these purposes within his mind for the purposes of making a public
broadcast, he had no idea of how they might be resolved, nor indeed was
he much interested in whether his various high-sounding public promises
gave the new Council any long-term coherent purpose. Like his successors, when faced with the obvious conflicts, he smoothed them
over—"Let every part of England be merry in its own way", "Death to
Hollywood", "different parts of the country" must "again walk their
several ways"—evasive metaphors that wriggle down the years, evidence
of a continuous refusal to confront real difficulties. What seems to interest
Keynes is the assumption of power. So he is insistent that above everything there must be some "proper part" for the state, and hence for the
Arts Council, to play. In order to achieve this overriding end, hostages
can be given to all parties, friendly or hostile, and the cultural history of
Britain may be distorted to show the "need" for state intervention. He
could say for instance that "really suitable" buildings for the arts had
"never been there" in Britain, ever. The nobility of the enterprise justifies the shady means.

Keynes also said that "The position today of artists of all sorts is disastrous." That also was offered as an *ex-cathedra* verdict, without evidence
of any kind. So what did he mean by "disastrous"? He could not have
meant that artists were starving—the years after the war were boom years
for artists of all kinds. Nor could he have meant, surely, that people were
paying no attention to artists' work—the same years were years of huge
audiences, everywhere, record use of libraries, vast listening figures for
the B.B.C.'s music and drama.

On the surface the assertion that public entertainers, and artists of all
kinds, were in dire straits, is as big a nonsense as the statement that pre-
war Britain's hundreds of theatres, halls, galleries, museums and libraries

were "not worth counting". Both statements would seem to come, not
from a notably clear mind, but from a mind dangerously uninfluenced
by evidence. Unless of course the terms are all being used with a special
meaning—a special meaning that harmonizes with the belief that for the
market economy to give unprecedentedly good wages to artists is a
crime—one of the "worser crimes" of present-day capitalism, and the
belief that "anything" would be better than "the present situation".

Suppose that the special meaning was this. Suppose that Keynes was
really saying that only those buildings built and approved by a state arts
body were worth counting? And suppose that he is really saying that it is
better, less criminal and less disastrous to have a state-approved artist on a
state grant, attracting little popular attention, than it is to have artists paid
for by the public in an open market? Then both of his statements become, given the new definitions, true. By such a definition the position of
Pope, Hogarth, Dickens, Elgar, and Auden was disastrous too, and none
of Britain's great libraries, nor the theatres of Garrick, Vestris, Bancroft,
Irving or Tree were "worth counting".

And if the higher purpose of the Arts Council was to impose the will of
the state—the state in the form, here, of the new Arts Council—upon a
fractious and dangerous arts world, then what did it matter that its overt
purposes were muddled and contradictory? The new Council would
exist in perpetuity, that was what mattered. It could then emphasize any
one of its seven smaller purposes when it suited its larger aim, and could
leave the others on the shelf. By this way of thinking, sustaining the Arts
Council becomes the same thing as sustaining the arts, and "state patronage of the arts" means simply state patronage of the Arts Council.

In practice the youthful Arts Council pursued only two of the seven
goals Keynes had suggested. It became the agency for state patronage of
the performing arts (the state continued to give direct grant aid to the
national museums and galleries), and it worked in a limited way as a
leveller. From the start it set up Scottish and Welsh Regional Offices, and
maintained the Regional Offices which C.E.M.A. had put in place; there
were efforts made to "disperse" excellence around the provinces, partly
by means of subsidized touring companies and partly through the subsidy of provincial orchestras and repertory companies.

The Arts Council's clients were all non-profit-distributing charitable
companies. Upon receiving their projected budgets the Council offered
them grant aid, which was to be paid at the year's end upon the receipt of
audited accounts showing that a loss of the required level had been made.
In effect the Council's clients were cushioned against the effects of making a modest loss, and were thus encouraged to undertake innovative or
experimental projects, or were permitted to try to attract "new" audi-

ences. There is plenty of evidence that it worked quite well for some
organizations in the first decades. Many of them did not in fact have to
call upon the sums set aside to "cushion" them, and others, while
accepting grant aid, did more adventurous work. In the case of the
repertory companies, grant aid enabled some of them to leave the tread-
mill of weekly rep, and to move to longer runs, with an improvement in
the technical standards of their work. By the early fifties, the Arts Council had eighteen such clients, nine of which were running "fortnightly
rep", and three with runs of three weeks or longer. (Of the 130 other,
unsubsidized, companies, only five had a fortnight or longer rehearsal
time.)

The disadvantages of this system are however obvious enough. The
first is that it is a system which is organization-centred. From first to last
the Arts Council has always been uneasy about giving support direct to
artists. It has always felt happier in dealing with organizations, whose
accountability is more readily checked upon, and this has meant that the
arts which exist only in ensemble work—which have organizations at
their core—have inevitably drawn more and more of the Arts Council
monies. In 1955 the Council gave 8% of its total grant to Drama
organizations; by 1975 it was 35%.

A second drawback to this system is that it doubly disadvantages those
art forms in which the organizations make profits by promoting work
which is commercially viable but second-rate. In such areas the genuine
artist will be in difficulties, although the economic state of the art overall
will seem healthy. One example of this lies in the visual arts, where the
sale of familiar pictures by the commercial organizations makes the
financial pages of the newspapers, but in which only a handful of prac-
tising artists of any quality make a living. A second example is in Literature, where publishing conglomerates return profits in the tens of
millions while good contemporary writers are largely unpublished and
almost totally unread. The Arts Council system offered no way out of
these problems. In 1970 the Arts Council gave a total of £199,477 to
Literature, which was less than a quarter of the Council's general operating costs. (In 1955 it did not even consider Literature, in its terms, an art
at all.)

The third problem of the system might be termed the disadvantages of
scale. When the annual grant to any organization was at most a few
thousand pounds, organizations could afford to gamble on being successful and on not relying on the grant. They could also afford, if their
gamble failed, to wait for the money until the books had been audited at
the end of the year. By 1959, however, the government grant to the Arts
Council exceeded £1,000,000, and the Council's major clients could not

afford to wait for their much larger grants without crippling themselves with the bank charges on their overdrafts. So the larger grants had to be paid month by month. In order to qualify, these organizations had to show, in effect, that they were on course for the planned deficit. Thus all possibility of not having to call upon the state grant was removed, and perforce administrators of subsidized companies settled into a routine in which they could not make an unanticipated profit, and in which they were inevitably drawn into dependency upon the state. The system ruled out what had been one of Keynes's possible purposes for the Council, acting as a pump primer.

Collectively, these drawbacks imposed a degree of inertia upon the system. Once an organization was a client, it was very difficult for the Council to shed it, or indeed radically to alter the terms of its support. Application for the following year's grant aid was made in the course of the year in which the client was receiving monthly support, and so organizations had to depart very far from the Council's embrace in order to lose their privileges.

Most important of all, those privileges included what Council officers actually called a Council "seal of approval". Gradually but inexorably, the Arts Council began to define its clients, collectively, as "the arts world", and the unsubsidized arts as "the popular arts", "entertainment", "amateur arts", "pastimes" or some other mildly derogatory epithet. By 1960 one had to ask a very odd question. Did the Arts Council, apart from its own bureaucratic definition ("the arts consist of state-supported cultural organizations"), actually know what the arts were?

The view of the arts in London's W.1. has often been a peculiar one. Here for example is the picture which Raymond Williams says the wartime Minister of Education, "Buck" de la Warr, had:

> He had Venetian visions of a post-war Lord Mayor's Show on the Thames in which the Board of Education led the arts in triumph from Whitehall to Greenwich in magnificent barges and gorgeous gondolas; orchestra, madrigal singers, Shakespeare from the Old Vic, ballet from Sadler's Wells, shining canvases from the Royal Academy, folk dancers from village greens—in fact Merrie England.

Well, at all events, Merrie Inner London. This picture of "the arts"—one that many metropolitan gurus carried with them for twenty years, before it was painted over with a much more horrible vision—sees civilized Britain as more or less contained within the centre of the capital, and outside, hanging about in a rather mangelwurzly way on their village greens, a few peasants bravely making do with amateur revelry.

Keynes said in his 1945 broadcast that the general enjoyment of the public was entirely compatible with the promotion of "traditional and contemporary arts in their noblest forms"; his later vision included the People's Palace and the Opera House, ballet and dancing on the village green. It therefore comes as a surprise to see that the Arts Council's 1946 Royal Charter speaks of "the fine arts exclusively" and to see that in practice the early Arts Council defined these so narrowly that for twenty years it altogether excluded poetry and the novel.

Then, in 1951, the year of the Festival of Britain, the Council accepted an additional £200,000 from government to grant-aid local activities (some rural, many amateur) some of which were very far removed from the apparently narrowly defined purposes of its new Charter.[6] Thus for one summer the Arts Council, with its new Charter to help develop "greater knowledge, understanding and practice of the fine arts exclusively", included such rural capering within their elevated remit, but still excluded the entirety of English literature.

What the Council grant-aided and what it approved of seemed partly to be a matter of historical accident, and partly the bureaucrat's natural preference for dealing with an organization rather than with anything so unpredictable as a live artist; but its overall actions bore little relation to the spread of purposes set out in the 1945 broadcast. Keynes's blurring of the lines between entertainment and art, for example, was forgotten for twenty years. W. E. Williams (now Secretary of the Arts Council, and now Sir William Emrys Williams C.B.E.) announced firmly in 1956 that "the distinction must be drawn between art and entertainment," adding the rider—an echo of a quite different Keynsian belief that art was prostituted by the market place—that favoured Arts Council clients were "interested in art and not in business".

The remarks were in reply to a letter from Dingle Foot, who had tried to enlist the Arts Council's support in getting the Entertainments Tax lifted from all theatres.[7] Williams refused to help in the campaign on the grounds that the state-aided theatres, which received grant aid and did not pay the tax, would be harmed by enhanced competition from a tax-free commercial theatre. "The arts" were thus firmly divided now from entertainment. They were uncommercial and loftily uninvolved in business. Most of all, they were distinguished, saved from commercial prostitution, by being state subsidized. Indeed, the Arts Council seemed more or less indifferent as to what "the arts" actually were—dance? films? poetry? novels? dancing on the village green?—and never seemed concerned that what was and what was not "art" in their eyes varied from year to year. Instead the Council concentrated upon institutionalizing its own authority, and emphasizing the correctness of its own methods of "support" for subsidized organizations—whatever they happened to do. In later letters to Foot, Williams made the Arts Council's self-interest unblushingly clear:

> It is our business... to look after our own chicks. Parliament has accepted the principle of protecting non-profit-distributing companies, and it is with these that the Arts Council is concerned. We are, in that sense, a vested interest... .

An organization with a vested interest in its own organization, a body more interested in developing its own bureaucratic arm muscles than in considering upon what it should or should not lay its hands. An organization that seemed too ready loftily to term its own expedient practices "principles". An organization which was thus more or less indifferent to the fact that it was excluding from the Arts Council's clutch of state-fed chickens all the nations's architects, its politicians, its philosophers, clowns, priests, orators, novelists and its poets.

*   *   *

In their slim book *The Arts in England*, published in 1947, the Arts Council's first post-war Secretary, Mary Glasgow, and her co-author, Professor Ifor Evans, accurately point to the financial freedom which the new Council enjoyed:

> A body which is not part of the formal machinery of government need not conform to official regulations and is in practice free to distribute the money allocated to it as it may decide, according to the particular needs of the time and the emergencies that may arise and not according to rules established by law and precedent.

They do not, however, draw attention to the freedom the new Council had to make perverse and private judgements, and to present them as meeting "the needs of the time". For the cultural "needs" of a time, even the "particular needs", may not be read off some cultural scale by trained sociologists, or even by dedicated arts officers. Needs, whether particular or general, do not exist "out there", though they may become real when we recognize them within our own experience—when for example we read D. H. Lawrence talking about living in our cities in "Nottinghamshire and the Mining Country":

> Now though perhaps nobody knew it, it was ugliness which betrayed the spirit of man, in the nineteenth century. The great crime which the moneyed classes and promoters of industry committed in the palmy Victorian days was the condemning of the

workers to ugliness, ugliness, ugliness: ugly religion, ugly hope, ugly love, ugly clothes, ugly furniture, ugly houses, ugly relationship between workers and employers. The human soul needs actual beauty even more than bread. ...

Do away with it all, then. At no matter what cost, start in to alter it. Never mind about wages and industrial squabbling. Turn the attention elsewhere. Pull down my native village to the last brick. Plan a nucleus. Fix the focus. Make a handsome gesture of radiation from the focus. And then put up big buildings, handsome, that sweep to a civic centre.

This demands an urgent personal response. By contrast, when Evans and Glasgow talk about our cities, and urban planning, and arts centres, it does not seem that they are really talking to the reader, and nothing they write connects with our personal experience:

By way of summing up, the hope may be repeated that the machinery of the private trust or the independent society may be used increasingly by all parties as a means of enlisting support from the rates and at the same time support from the Arts Council, while providing as wide as possible a field for the activities of artists and performers outside the dangers of monopoly control in the commercial world, and making possible a form of management which is both expert and politically disinterested.

From the point of view of the community itself, a vigorous arts club can be a channel to make known local needs and wishes and to draw up a programme for each season which shall be well balanced and acceptable, not simply dependent upon the convenience of those who have something to sell and are offering plays, concerts or exhibitions from a London selection.

The language here—uncertain yet pompous, as if the authors are not talking to their fellow citizens but shouting nervously from the top of distant Olympus—is typical of the worst kind of early Arts Council writing. It seems to be offering a description of the ways artists and audiences should meet, but it is impossible to imagine anything real happening as a result of it. It expects no response. It is a bureaucratic style which offers a glum foretaste of decades of reports, surveys, strategies and discussion papers on the arts written in the same drear jargon.

Until the early eighties Arts Council writing continued to have the same inbuilt, unexplained hostility to "the commercial world" and those "who have something to sell"—those, that is, who are promoting art that pleases a substantial number of people—and as usual it is pepped up by muscular terms—*expert, enlisting support, vigorous*—that disguise the lacklustre thing that is being described.

The appeal is made always to some unknowable abstraction—"the point of view of the community itself"—which, the reader seems to be assured, is something that Arts Council bureaucrats can recognize and evaluate, even though you (a member of "the community itself", no less) may not know what its single point of view is. Likewise, who is to decide what is a "well-balanced and acceptable" programme? (The locals cannot decide. How would they know whether it was well-balanced; which parts of the programme should be acceptable to which parts of the community? Obviously the only person capable of arbitrating on the programme is the detached observer, the officer of the state.)

The Arts Council's language from its earliest days is carefully weighted with terms that imply hearty communal participation in the promotion of the subsidized arts. *The community* has *perceived demands* and *takes initiatives* to *develop* the arts *in partnership* with local authorities, and gains a new *identity* from each *success*—but what actually happens, as subsidized art is dispersed around the country, is that it seems to exist in a different realm from the lives local people live and the work local artists actually do.

More important still, the language of the Arts Council is incapable of discussing actual life in any part of Britain, save in an arts bureaucrat's office. And nowhere, nowhere at all, can we ever see the forming of a genuine critical judgement. The Arts Council is forever set apart from genuine criticism by its absolute insistence upon the secrecy that surrounds its judgements. That dialogue between critic and spectator, or between critic and reader ("'This is so, isn't it?' 'Yes, but...'") was always absent because the Arts Council appointed panels that worked in secrecy, which did not publish any explanation of their judgements and which did not engage in creative argument.

So the Arts Council habitually described the subsidized arts world as if that was British culture, pronounced its judgements superior to those offered by critics, and described its own operation in such terms as seemed to attribute every cultural value exclusively to the state-aided world. The effect of all this upon the language of the arts has been incalculably depressing. Terms such as *the best, excellence, judgement,* and *standards,* which once belonged to the genuine critic, have been submerged by their insistent misuse by the Arts Council in a pond of journalese, and those waters have recently been muddied further by the Council's throwing in its own dreary management jargon: *client assessment, networking, community needs, development* and *management strategies.* It has thus become difficult to talk about the arts in Britain without seeming to adopt some at least of the Arts Council's attitudes, and hence quite difficult not to talk simple gibberish.

* * *

Meanwhile the Arts Council got rid of the only woman on its senior staff, and became an all-male, all-white, middle-aged metropolitan brotherhood. From Clark's account, the motive for the Council's man of bottom sacking Mary Glasgow seems to have been what holders of the male conspiracy theory might suspect. Her sex prevented her from being, so to speak, one of them:

> During one of our visits to Portugal Maynard Keynes had died, and most people imagined that I would succeed him as chairman of the Arts Council. I confess that I expected to do so, and rather looked forward to the prospect.... But the Treasury have a principle that a volatile chairman, and in Keynes' case a brilliant one, should be succeeded by what the eighteenth century used to call "a man of bottom"; and they discovered an amiable example in Sir Ernest Pooley, who was Warden of the Draper's Company. Having no interest in the arts he could be relied on not to press their claims too strongly. ...
>
> A year or two later I asked leave to retire from the Arts Council for a year or two. I had been chairman of the Art Panel for almost ten years, and thought that the Panel would benefit from a change. I was lucky to be away at that time because Pooley came to the conclusion that there should also be a change in the general directions, and set himself to get rid of Miss Glasgow. How this was achieved I never asked; it must have been a painful process, as the Arts Council was her whole life and, although sometimes a little governessy, she seemed to me to carry out her duties in an exemplary manner.[8]

She was succeeded, inevitably, by W. E. Williams.[9] His deputy was Mr M. J. McRobert, the Assistant Secretary General Mr E. W. White, the Finance Officer Mr D. P. Lund, and the directors for drama, music and art were, respectively, Mr J. Moody, Mr J. Denison and Mr P. James. From 1947 to 1952 the Arts Council also had a post of "Associate Drama Director", whose occupant, Mr C. Landstone, was also General Manager of the Bristol Theatre Royal. His recollections convey something of the male, clubbish, common-room feel of Williams's Arts Council, and of its desire less to promote the arts in general than to promote its own authority and its own consistency:

The sixth Annual Report of the Arts Council, the first under
W. E. Williams's Secretaryship, appeared in November, 1951. Let
me repeat in print what I told him at the time. I consider that it was
the most disastrous document which ever came from the Council.
It dealt with the conflicting questions of "Raise or Spread".... .
The report made no categorical statements of new policy; but, by
raising a number of "Rosa Dartle"-like questions, it damaged all
the work of the previous ten years.[10]

The "work" had been to smooth over the Arts Council's conflicting
aims. The "disaster" was just that it did harm to the Council's public
relations by calling attention to what some of the words might actually
mean. That Williams may, in his naîveté, have been seeking a truthful
answer to some genuinely difficult questions, did not exonerate him from
the charge of damaging "the cause".

He quickly learned the Arts Council's coded language however, and by
1956, when he wrote an Arts Council pamphlet called *The First Ten Years*
he had further narrowed the area in which high standards and excellence
could be found. The lustre of excellence now shone only from subsidized
performing arts companies in London and the larger cities:

> The Arts Council believes, then, that the first claim upon its atten-
> tion and assistance is that of maintaining in London and the larger
> cities effective power houses of opera, music and drama; for unless
> these quality institutions can be maintained the arts are bound to
> decline into mediocrity. ...
>
> The achievement and preservation of standards in the arts is,
> primarily, then, the role of the professional, just as the task of
> diffusing the arts outside the cities is largely the business of the
> amateur.

This further narrowing of focus—amateurs now have a walk-on part
only, with little chance of helping to set any standards, while people
living in the smaller cities would seem now to live in art-free zones—is
achieved by another persuasive redefinition of the term "the arts".
Wrapped up in one of the metaphors for which Williams was notorious
comes the news that unless quality institutions, "power houses", can be
maintained in London for each of the arts, then each in turn will decline
into mediocrity. Without the Bloomsbury Group English letters shrivel
to dust. Without a National Theatre repertory collapses.

Electrical metaphors in Arts Council prose are third favourites to
metaphors drawn from gardening (easily the winner) and those of the
battlefield. The Arts Council sometimes suggests that it sees itself as a
private army, happiest when the chaps are tramping through the rose

garden waving their battery chargers. But the electrical metaphor has a particular point here. If the power house fails, then all the lights on the national grid (as officers came to call the touring circuits) will go out. Who then are seeing themselves as having their hands on the great cultural switch?

Those power houses become at other times jewels in the Arts Council's crown, roses in their garden and, more prosaically, "centres of excellence". Each image suggests that the subsidized arts are possessed by the metropolitan mandarins, and contain an exclusive elixir of splendour, which the Arts Council may benevolently distribute—providing, that is, that we give due obeisance to the biggest jewel and the loveliest rose of them all.

The Arts Council thus spent a significant part of its formative years establishing and consolidating its position. Its major weapon was a new kind of pseudo-critical language that described its actions in terms of "demand" and "needs" and "provision" and other words more commonly used in the welfare services. It was at times unbearably narcissistic. It started to talk of "the arts world" as if it were no longer what artists did, but as if it were what arts bureaucrats, and in particular the officers of the Arts Council, chose to do.

3

Confirmation

The publication of the 1965 White Paper *Policy for the Arts; the First Steps* was widely considered, at least by its promoters and those who reacted in the press, to be a momentous event. It was hailed as evidence that the state "recognized the importance" of the arts, as if things become more important when politicians talk about them. It was generally agreed to be an "advance" to have the state publishing an official document on the subject, irrespective of whether the document made any sense or not.

Among other things the White Paper proposed that the government's annual grant to the Arts Council should be increased. The Council could then make larger grants in its turn to the regional associations, to leading artistic enterprises in Scotland and Wales and to "certain specialized projects". The Council warmly welcomed its publication therefore, and set itself up immediately as the main agency through which the White Paper's proposals would be made reality, in time talking so proprietorially about it that anyone might suppose the White Paper's sole purpose was to support and expand the Arts Council. Yet the Paper's general tone and many of its arguments were at odds with the direction the Council had been taking, and the majority of its conclusions—about museums, the education system and the work of the local authorities, all of which the White Paper discussed at length—were well outside the Arts Council's interests.

Most interestingly, however, the Council was asked to make a start on what had been at its birth its most urgent priority. Twenty years after Keynes had said that it would be "our biggest problem", there was to be a small Housing the Arts Fund administered by the Arts Council.

The White Paper began:

> 1 The relationship between artist and State in a modern democratic community is not easily defined. No one would wish State patronage to dictate taste or in any way restrict the liberty of even the most unorthodox and experimental of artists.
>
> 2 But if a high level of artistic achievement is to be sustained and the best in the arts made more widely available, more generous

and discriminating help is urgently needed, locally, regionally and nationally.

It was obviously inconceivable to the White Paper's authors that there might be no single relationship between "artist" and "State". Nor was anyone churlish enough at the time to suggest that formulation of such a meaningless abstraction was in any case a task not worth attempting. It was plainly beyond argument that "the artist" needed help, and beyond argument that it was the state that had to give it, locally, regionally and nationally.

Keynes's blurring of the boundary between entertainment and art was, however, back in favour. We were no longer to be concerned with "the fine arts exclusively" but with popular enjoyment. Indeed, there was more than a hint that the very best civic arts centres had been slyly doing the work of the People's Palaces on the side:

> 8   Centres that succeed in providing a friendly meeting ground where both light entertainment and cultural projects can be enjoyed help also to break down the isolation from which both artist and potential audience have suffered in the past.

So, with one of those unnerving shifts in the official line with which arts administrators in Eastern Europe are familiar, those in subsidized organizations who had been guiltily disobeying the instructions of the Arts Council's apparatchiks, and had not been promoting the fine arts exclusively, suddenly found themselves smiled upon by the great and the good.

More unsettling still, those reinstated dissidents found themselves offered as role models for arts administrators throughout the land. For the White Paper, in spite of its protestations that state patronage must not dictate taste, nevertheless soon made it clear that its plans for every part of Britain were no less comprehensive than Williams's had been in wartime or than Mussolini's had been in pre-war Italy[1]:

> 9   Another encouraging trend is the growing recognition of the importance of strengthening contacts between regional and civic arts associations in different parts of the country.
>
> 10   But we have a long way to go before effective associations of this kind become common form everywhere.

Everywhere!—Keynes's word again!—although the customary sop is given to provincial sensibilities, albeit with a slightly surly twist. Keynes had been generous in spirit, if a mite vacuous: "Let every part of Merry England be merry in its own way." The White Paper is more grudging:

> 10   ... Of course no provincial centre can hope to rival the full wealth and diversity of London's art treasures, but each can

have something of its own that is supreme in some particular field.

If that means anything at all, it means W. E. Williams's Arts Council dogma—that the state must above all support the metropolitan "power houses", without which the arts are bound to decline into mediocrity—had been questioned and overthrown. Each place—each provincial centre, small towns? villages even?—could now have something that is supreme. Notice too the tight-lipped but determined openness of the word *something*. Provincial centres can step outside the Arts Council's recent parameters for the "fine arts exclusively". Dancers on the village green could now be an approved something. The something could even be a poet.

The White Paper did contain two other novel ideas. First, it suggested that the secret of making arts buildings successful was to paint them in bright colours. Those buildings that "failed to move with the times" have a "cheerless unwelcoming air". "No greater disservice can be done to the serious artist than to present his work in an atmosphere of old-fashioned gloom and undue solemnity." And, as a way of providing "much-needed colour":

> 54 ...Enterprising localities might well investigate the possibility of mobile arts centres[1] and travelling theatres. This means growing accustomed to some of the latest developments in building techniques. Temporary inflatable structures are already in use in industry. All that is needed is to find models that can be given the gay "Come to the Fair" atmosphere essential for recreational purposes.

And then, in summary:

> 100 Nor can we ignore the growing revolt, especially among the young, against the drabness, uniformity and joylessness of much of the social furniture we have inherited from the industrial revolution. This can be directed, if we so wish, into making Britain a gayer and more cultivated country.

Which brings us to the White Paper's second new idea. In paragraph 100 it is, you will note, the young who are especially revolting. But in 1965 the young are everything:

> 7 ...A younger generation, however, more self-confident than their elders...are more hopeful material. They will want gaiety and colour, informality and experimentation.
> 59 ...Many of them have a natural talent for painting and drawing, and for making things, that surprises their parents.
> 61 ...The imagination and free flow of some of the writing

in prose and poetry, the quality of some of the painting and pot-
tery, and the high standard of some of the choral singing and of the
orchestral playing, culminating in the National Youth Orchestra,
outshine the achievements of any previous generation.

    62   ... There are schools built since 1945 where children have
shown how they appreciate and respect well-designed buildings,
enlivened by the occasional mural or piece of sculpture, stimulating
colours... and skilful landscaping.

There in paragraph 62 is the essence of the White Paper's view of the
world. Providing we supply the young with brightly coloured state
buildings, erected within the Arts Council's lifetime (before then, presumably, there were no educational establishments worth counting), we
can leave it all to them, with their gaiety, colour, informality and experimentation.

Informality and experimentation! Can any government publication in
history have tried to curry favour with the young quite as abjectly as this?
"They will want," it says—not "They will need," not even that pretence—"They will want gaiety and colour, informality and experimentation." So it must of course be given to them. The state has a duty to give
them all they want. And the significance the state attaches to such experimentation will surprise their parents, who did not in their day see
childhood play elevated to the status of art.

There were sceptics at the time, of course, who saw the self-confidence
of the young as arrogance, their informality as slackness of mind and
their gaiety as evidence of temporary derangement. Not Jennie Lee,
however. For her the hippies of the sixties, the "alternative cultures", the
flower power houses, the sit-ins at which the young demonstrated their
appreciation and respect for their brightly coloured educational institutions, were "more hopeful material" than the post-war generation. In
every way the Flower Power people were better than their elders.

*   *   *

The White Paper, like previous utterances by the Arts Council itself,
warned the young against earning their livings by selling their work
directly to the public, and thus falling into prostitution. Capitalism
offered too easy pickings to an informal young experimenter. However,
the state is now wise to the evil ways of the free market:

    7   ... There is no reason why attractive presentation should be
left to those whose primary concern is with quantity and profitability.

Why should the Devil have all the bright packages? Could not the Arts
Council, under its prestigious new chairman, Lord Goodman (G of the

Arts Council) respond to the young, with their colourful ways and their bright new alternative culture? In the Arts Council report of 1966–7 the chairman modestly offered hope that the Arts Council would be able to widen the scope of its response, and acknowledged that Britain could have, in each locality, something that was supreme in some particular field:

> We do not exist to plan artistic and cultural projects. Very few are the fruit of direct Arts Council labours. And this is as it should be. The larger the extent of national subsidy, the more vital that it should neither bear nor seem to bear the imprint of a single body. Artistic life in this country must not be dominated by a small non-elected appointed caucus in St James's Square. The avoidance even of the possibility of such domination is a conscious part of our policy. Thus we encourage the development of a sensible region-alism—not the "fragmentation" of established important insti-tutions or the notion that every town must have an opera house...

As is its invariable custom, the Arts Council had set up a Committee of Inquiry into "the needs of opera and ballet throughout the nation", and, not for the first or the last time, another committee, under the chair-manship of Sir William Emrys Williams, to investigate "the needs of drama". (Goodman's own report on the needs of the four London orchestras, another old favourite, mentioned in the White Paper, was published in 1970, and was to provide a valuable reference for all sub-sequent enquiries into the same problem.)

The 1966–7 Report gives an impression of an Arts Council now a "well-established institution", equipped with a government grant of £5,700,000 a year, preparing to let a hundred flowers bloom. Yet could those new and different flowers "in some field" be judged on the same scale of excellence as those forced in the metropolitan power houses? The White Paper had seemed to urge a wider view of art, a movement away from the Arts Council's narrow view of "the fine arts exclusively", and the 1967 Charter removed reference to exclusivity and spoke simply of "the arts". The new Charter had as its objects:

> to develop and improve the knowledge, understanding and prac-tice of the arts; to increase the accessibility of the arts to the public throughout Great Britain; and to advise and co-operate with Government Departments, Local Authorities and other bodies on any matters concerned whether directly or indirectly with the foregoing objects.

From that time the Council also received its annual Grant through the Department of Education and Science.

Yet, in 1967, the upper echelons of the Council are doubting whether the colourful flowers blooming around the country really count as art. Could "quality" really exist in the provinces or in the unsubsidized areas, in the activities of Local Authorities or amongst the experimentally-minded young? "How shall we reconcile the diffusion of money and effort with the maintenance of quality?"

The dilemma was seen to be at its most critical in the drama. Here was a field in which the best often seemed to come from the unsubsidized sector. As the Arts Council increasingly saw state subsidy as the imprimatur of the best, should they try to find a way of subsidizing what was already profitable, or should they, in the case of the theatre, give their "seal of approval" to the second-best which seemed to need state support? The question seemed to be firmly answered. "The English Theatre flourished under private management before we were dreamed of," said Goodman firmly. "It is our duty, in the administration of subsidy, to co-operate with the best elements." So that much is clear. Public support should ally itself with the best elements in theatre, which meant some private managements (and, presumably, the same applied to publishing, folk singing, variety, jazz, circus and much else). Yet Goodman then voices a strange ideological doubt: "Whether we can *or should* in the end give direct aid to private managements is a problem we are now investigating." (My italics) If the flourishing theatres of private managements provided "the best elements" in that field, what ideological constraints should prevent the Arts Council, if asked, from supporting them? Why should the Council not support *the best elements* when they were developed by local authorities, by youthful record promoters, by profitable publishing concerns? What are these hidden constraints? What could they be, except a determination to sustain the Arts Council's definition of "the arts" as being that which they subsidize, and a determination to elevate the expedient systems of grant-aiding, worked out in the Council's formative years, to the status of principles?

That persuasive redefinition of "the arts", so insidiously promoted by the Council over so many years, is at the root of both the wider problems the Council has caused to British cultural life, and of the Council's internal tensions. That which receives subsidy is presumed to be in need of state assistance either because it is *avant-garde* and a paying audience cannot yet be found for it, or, if it is plainly not *avant-garde* at all (like Shakespeare or classical opera), it is either made to be so (by being presented in ridiculous "experimental" productions) or presumed to be the victim of inflationary pressures which, because the arts are "labour-intensive", supposedly mean that costs must always outrun receipts even from large audiences.

Yet of course both of these (dubious) propositions are just as true of cultural activities which do not receive any subsidy at all. A circus is no less labour-intensive than a touring play, and a theme park no less than an arts centre. Yet comparison of the economics of subsidized and commercial would not have mattered much if the Arts Council had not collected its lists of clients by a series of historical chances, and then spoken of those eclectic groupings as if they contained exclusively within them all "quality", all "excellence" and all "standards" in "the arts". And it would have mattered even less if the Arts Council had not implied so often that the quality, excellence and standards came from the Arts Council itself, rather than from the artist. It was as if the Milk Marketing Board had announced that only white liquid receiving their regular subsidy could be classed as milk, and as if the Board had also hinted rather more surprisingly that its own officials had personally serviced all the country's worthwhile cattle.

*   *   *

Goodman's Arts Council had two arms. There was one which held the Arts Council's jewels (its power houses, its centres of excellence, benchmarks of quality, its roses), in its grip. The other arm groped for local initiatives, fumbled for distinctive and different "somethings" in each locality, reacted to the colourful young and looked to hand over responsibility when it was able. The first arm spread its bright metropolitan wares about the land, and arranged tours so that the provinces might see great ballet, opera, drama and exhibitions which were essentially of London. That arm waved the flag of decentralization. The second, encouraging cultural ferment everywhere, was concerned with the devolution of financial and managerial control. Goodman's reports (like most others) made guarded reference to the fact that synchronizing the two limbs was not an easy task, yet the reports seemed to say that the Council could be uniquely responsible and responsive, could maintain rigorous standards yet insist upon the right to fail, and could be an agent both of decentralization and of devolution. Goodman hinted that the secrets of these administrative miracles were contained within the inner sanctum of the Council. He, as Chairman, had been privy to these mysteries, and was thus endowed with magical powers to fuse all the Council's conflicting intentions:

> I would wish that there might be a million Arts Councils in this country—so that there might be a million men who enjoy the benefits of training as their Chairmen. There is no more liberal education in the whole wide world. In six years of enthralling office I have—unlike the Bourbons—learnt more and forgotten more

than in any period of my life. A Chairman of the Arts Council finds
that every preconception in relation to the administration of the
arts is either mistaken or at least calls for massive qualification. If
the wicked can ever hope for leisure, I shall hope one day to write
at greater length on this theme.[2]

Yet elsewhere the report suggests that the old Arts Council of "the fine
arts exclusively" has not found it easy to accommodate to the wider
vision of "the arts" that the White Paper promoted. It seemed to some
that Merrie England (each merry in his own way) was come again—but
Goodman was much more curmudgeonly:

> Certainly enthusiastic groups of young people are working under
> totally unorthodox conditions in a fashion which they find deeply
> satisfying. They are producing plays and playlets and entertain-
> ments without the inhibition of formal stages, curtains, proscenia
> and the like. They are desperately seeking to break away from
> conventional restrictions.... But misgivings and doubts will al-
> ways be felt by my age group. It would be hypocrisy to pretend
> that the young have our total trust.

The Arts Council is seemingly now embodied in Lord Goodman. (First
the Council speaks with the voice of his "age group", then seems to be G
himself: the "our" in "our total trust" is splendidly ambivalent.) And
Goodman, and the Arts Council, seem both determined to belittle the
significance of what the White Paper had helped to unleash. For the new
arts activities of the sixties—however childish, however drab, whatever
their merits and demerits may have been—cannot be described as if they
are nothing more than adolescent tinkerings with the conventions of the
nineteenth-century proscenium stage. There was a plethora of new writing, in novels, poetry and for the stage. There were ambitious statements
made in new realms, in conceptual and abstract art, in photography and
film. There was widespread experimentation—for good or ill—in choreo-
graphy, in acting and directing, and (most particularly) in popular music.
And very many of those concerned with the "new and experimental"—David Bailey, John Lennon, the Establishment Club and *Private Eye*, Nems Enterprises Ltd, Paul McCartney, Mary Quant, Roy and
John Boulting, Jean Shrimpton and the Rolling Stones, say—were
succeeding commercially, without benefit of state subsidy.

The Arts Council, in the person of Lord Goodman, chose to pretend
that all of this was merely a matter of a few youngsters tinkering with
theatrical convention, in distant parts of the country (it being understood
that they, the Arts Council, the custodians of the nation's culture, were
inevitably at the centre of things):

But we had, rightly or wrongly, heard that a group of youngsters around the country had some new ideas and the rumour grew with disturbing persistence. Reverberations came from arts laboratories in London and nearby seaside resorts, from towns rarely associated with artistic explosions. From all over the place reports of quaint new phenomena were raced to us by carrier-pigeon, mule and camel. We sat at the gates of the Arts Council to receive them, feverishly unwrapping the messages and reporting them back to our colleagues.

In truth, the Council was afraid—not least because so much of the youth frenzy of the sixties was a straightforward commercial success. The new photography, new music, new films, new design did not look as if it depended upon Arts Council monies. Keynes's argument that the artist needed state aid because he did not know his own direction seemed likely to be disproved by events. So the Council took the most decisive action of which it was capable. It set up a committee, "primed with a modest grant for its researches, and the Eldritch proceedings began." Yet even this bold bureaucratic action did not fend off the youth threat: "Meetings were invaded by demonstrators; they engaged in long and protracted arguments about protocol, propounded by citizens of terrifying solemnity, and clamourings for justice, meaning thereby a large share of our depleted funds." In other words youth was behaving much as the White Paper had, apparently, hoped. This was the "growing revolt" of the young, their "impatience" with the old order, the visible sign of their much-vaunted desire for "informality and experimentation".

The Arts Council had, it would seem, taken the new money offered by the government (the "depleted" 1966–7 government grant to the Council was a 46% increase on the previous year), but had not taken the clear advice of the White Paper:

> 92   ... New ideas, new values, the involvement of large sections of the community hitherto given little or no opportunity to appreciate the best in the arts, all have their place. It will take time for the Arts Council and other organizations working in this field to adjust their plans to the wider opportunities now offered them.

The Arts Council had not adjusted. It had merely accommodated to what it regarded as a threat by its usual procedures, which were set within its "firmly established" bureaucratic structures. It had created an "Experimental Projects Committee... to deal with applications from any activity which looks 'new' in the sense that it does not fit into the pattern of the other arts".

By this time the Arts Council had, just, admitted Literature to "the arts", but it still had no department of dance, or opera, or, come to that, film, weaving, folk song, clowning, puppetry, needlework, tapestry-making, *haute cuisine*, topiary, juggling, dressmaking, jazz, storytelling, architecture, rock, interior design or twenty other things which featured, rightly or wrongly, on the "Arts pages" of the newspapers. When Good-man spoke of "new" art, of things which didn't fit into "the pattern of the other arts", he meant things which didn't fit into the departments of the state Arts Council. And by suggesting that all those things which didn't fit into those categories were "new", he seemed to be saying that everything which did not fall into one of the post-war-subsidy grooves (only a small segment of the arts did) was an "experimental project", somewhat suspect and almost certainly inferior.

Miklos Haraszti, in *The Velvet Prison: Artists under State Socialism* (1983) writes of communist Hungary:

> Each artistic genre or art form is "represented" by a ministerial department, so that the boundaries between (permitted) art forms correspond to demarcations between bureaucracies.... Students who wish to become artists must choose their "occupation" from one of the approved art forms. The Ministerial departments elabor-ate their own aesthetics. Only accepted art forms are developed through innovation.[3]

His strictures could well have applied to Goodman's Arts Council, where all "experimental projects" brought to the Council's attention—anything that is which had no recent history of state support—would at best be the subject of a recommendation "despatched for an experimental period direct to the Council. The Council will examine these hybrids with care, and will decide about their support, receiving appropriate advice from appropriate advisers."

The British Arts Council consists, not of a "peer group" of artists, nor of arts critics, nor of arts academics, but of state appointees drawn from the great and the good and put there by the government's Minister of Arts. They are, very largely, laymen. "Appropriate advisers" can like-wise be anyone, from state bureaucrats to local politicians. The way in which the hybrids that fell through the bureaucratic mesh were dealt with in Britain does not therefore in one respect differ from the old Hungarian system. In neither case is there any guarantee that the work will be subjected to genuine criticism by a competent person. The hybrids will be judged according to political and bureaucratic criteria, with case law determined by narrow definitions of "art", of "excellence" and what is "experimental". As Haraszti says,

Each national culture introduces control by considering some genres as relics to be preserved. Naturally, this is done in order to "safeguard tradition". Thus, if one trespasses into certain unacceptable genres, one risks being thought not only antagonistic to the common good but also downright unpatriotic.

So the Arts Council passed through its third decade of life unable to respond to much that fell outside its own reach, but yet urging its own subsidized organs to "move with the times" and be "experimental". It faced the seventies therefore in the unhappy position of suffering—with arms of unequal length—simultaneously from constipation and from over-exertion.

4

Parentage

Reports spawn reports, and no part of British public life produces them with such evident relish as the state arts system. In the decade following the country's first (and only) White Paper on the arts, arts bureaucrats produced mountains of plans, surveys and reports for each other to read. With an enthusiasm which at times verged upon hysteria they wrote of revolution, discerned "rising demand" everywhere, and vied with each other in their clamour for increased state support for fashionable doings. The arts, it seemed (some actually said it), were now to be a state *service*, freely available to all, as glasses and teeth then were.

The Arts Council had in 1959 produced a survey *Housing the Arts in Great Britain*. Now that the Council was able to attend to Keynes's "first priority", the survey's eight general "rules" were exhumed and used in a plethora of further reports on the various "needs" of regions, cities and towns:

1   A region with 10 million inhabitants should have one permanent professional opera company.

2   A region with 5 million inhabitants should have one permanent symphony orchestra.

3   Towns of 150,000 or more should have one theatre large enough to house major touring productions including opera and ballet.

4   Towns of 100,000 or more should have one permanent repertory company, with its own theatre.

5   Towns of 75,000 or more should have one hall suitable for large symphony and choral concerts.

6   Towns of 50,000 or more should have one museum and/or art gallery, and one professionally staffed Arts Centre (in use all year).

7   Towns of 20,000 or more should have one Arts Centre which may be part of another establishment; one Music Club or Arts Society, presenting regular series of professional events; one amateur orchestra (on a scale of at least one for every 60,000 inhabitants); facilities for showing regular touring exhibitions.

8   Towns of 10,000 or more should have an amateur dramatic society, a Choral Society, and an Amateur Art Society or Club (each on a scale of at least one for every 30,000 inhabitants).

There has never been anything which demonstrated more plainly the Arts Council's London mind (the figures are subdivisions of the scale of provision in the capital) or its narrow view of what constitutes the arts. For here "the arts" comprise nothing but state-aided *organizations* and state-supported venues.

Yet we can live full and artistically satisfying lives without being touched by any of these state mechanisms and state services. Our "needs" may be for other things—for libraries, craft workshops, musical instruments in our homes, local dances, a garden, bookshops, or a drawing easel that we can set up and use without belonging to a state art society or club. A region which has the right proportion of state arts organizations and state-supported arts venues might please a Soviet planner (when the population of Riga was substantially increased the Soviet authorities solemnly added the necessary proportion of extra seats in the state opera house), but it may be spiritually dead. Judging against such a scale means that Wordsworth's Lake District, Burns's Scotland or Palmer's Shoreham would be sadly deficient. Yarmouth by contrast would score highly.

One publication which used these "rules" was *The Arts in the South*, a survey and report published in 1970, at the birth of the South's Regional Arts Association. Applying them to the South of England, the author prescribed the following:

(i)   Permanent repertory theatres with their own buildings in Portsmouth, Reading and Southampton.

(ii)   A large touring theatre in Southampton.

(iii)   Large concert halls in Havant, Poole, Reading and Swindon.

(iv)   Museum/Art Galleries in Havant, Gosport, Fareham, Crawley and Poole.

(v)   Portsmouth, Southampton, Bournemouth, Reading, Poole, Havant, Worthing, Gosport, Fareham and Crawley should have professionally staffed arts centres, in use all the year round.

(vi)   Maidenhead, Eastleigh, Farnborough, Aldershot, Salisbury, Basingstoke, Bognor Regis, Winchester, Christchurch, Windsor, Horsham, Newbury, Andover, Ryde and Chichester should have an arts centre which may be part of another establishment.

(vii)   Portsmouth, Havant, Fareham, Crawley, Eastleigh, Farnborough, Aldershot, Lymington, Bognor Regis, Christchurch and Ryde should have a music club or local arts society presenting a regular series of professional events.

(viii) Poole, Havant, Fareham, Farnborough, Basingstoke, Bognor Regis, Newbury, Andover and Ryde should have facilities for showing regular touring art exhibitions.

"These recommendations are valid in certain cases," the report and survey went on, adding rather obscurely, "but here they serve to provide an abstract framework against which to measure present provision of facilities, and a guideline to the real recommendations and conclusions in Section 12."

Section 12 makes many real recommendations, including that the new Regional Arts Association should extend its region to include West Surrey, and that it should write a series of further reports "on particular subjects". Mainly, however, it lists an impressive number of ways in which the new R.A.A. can spend money, including financial assistance to all the main public art galleries and to amateur arts societies, together with grants to local authorities to put sculpture "in public places"; grants to some theatres (and amateur drama societies), with guarantees against loss to others; grants to the Bournemouth Symphony Orchestra, and assistance to many other musical organizations, including the Eastern Authorities Orchestral Organization and the Worthing Municipal Orchestra; contributions towards the establishment of arts centres "where such amenities are planned", to local arts festivals "where they show artistic purpose", to "arts laboratories"[1] to assist them in buying "suitable premises", and for the establishment of "local arts councils" throughout the region.

Those were the real recommendations, and one must give thanks that no unreal ones were made, for the additional state expenditure proposed is already impressive. More state aid (or, to use the newly fashionable term, "public investment") is the answer to every cultural conundrum, as in the author's comments on the Bournemouth Symphony Orchestra:

> The orchestra incurred a deficiency of approximately £14,000 in 1968–9, and, unless support *by way of subsidy* is significantly increased this year, could face a loss of around £60,000 in 1969–70. [My italics]

Or, as it is more blatantly put in the report's conclusion: "It is clear from the present low level of public investment in the arts at both local and national level that something needs to be done."

It is clear then, that local authorities should now be given state money to put state-approved statues in their parks and cemeteries? clear that "arts laboratories" need to be given state money to buy suitably equipped premises for carrying out arts experiments, whatever they are? clear that when people decide to have a local festival they should be state-assisted, if the festival shows artistic "purpose"? All that follows, does it, from the "low level" of "public investment" in the arts?

First, what sort of sense does it make to talk of public investment, or state bribery, being at a "low level"? The phrase implies that there is a right and natural level which produces good art. As that same report lists an impressive amount of arts acitivity which had been going on in Southern Britain before it had the benefit of a Regional Arts Association (rather more impressive than a similar survey might now prove to be), what had been going wrong, and what made state money the only possible corrective? Why could the Bournemouth Symphony Orchestra not have charged their better-off patrons more, for example?

Is public investment said to be at a "low level" in comparison with some other countries? If so, then actual statistics are likely to confound the writer. Comparisons showing that the British government "spends less" on the arts than, say, France, often collapse because we too readily use the Arts Council bureaucrat's definition of what "the arts" are. Bring into the picture such things as spending on the arts within the education system, and spending on public libraries, and spending on the arts by the B.B.C., and you could have shown that Britain's state expenditure runs at too *high* a level. Conversely, a comparison with the United States which included spending on the arts in the state education budgets, and also included spending in each country's armed forces' budget (an area of high U.S. expenditure), would again show Britain's level to be "low".

No data compel us to increase or decrease state aid. We do it because there is a will to do it. Arts Council bureaucrats decided at the time that certain organizations and certain activities—some "festivals", "arts lab-oratories", arts centres in the planning stage, amateur operatic societies "when they perform opera as opposed to operetta and musical comedy" and sculpture in public places—were "art", and had "needs" which the state had a duty to meet. At the same time, and largely unremarked, other cultural activities in Britain were in decline. The larger theatre circuits had almost completely disappeared, the large touring circuses had collapsed, local bookshops were closing everywhere and cinema attendances were spiralling downwards. But none of this was Arts Coun-cil "art". And that some people obviously still wanted some of these things did not qualify them to be "needs". *The Arts in the South* was not then surveying the cultural lives of Southerners and drawing logical conclusions from carefully considered premises. It was instead looking narrowly at the extending and financing of state-approved organizations, venues and activities, concerned less with discovering the work of the artist than with establishing a role for the Arts Council and its satellites. What is "clear" from this, and many kindred documents, is that the people who wrote them wanted to be part of a growing new welfare-state bureaucracy.

*   *   *

The Arts Council's annual grant-in-aid from government rose from £13,725,000 in 1972–3 to £17,388,000 in 1973–4. Nearly £4m of this went to the Scottish and Welsh Arts Councils. Of the remainder more than £4m went to the four jewels in the crown: the Royal Opera House, the Sadler's Wells Trust (Coliseum) Ltd, the National Theatre Board and the Royal Shakespeare Theatre. A further £1·5m went to the Regional Arts Associations, some £0·6m to Housing the Arts, and the remainder to the Arts Council's 1,500 or so other direct-grant clients. The largest grant the Council made in that year was £2,195,000 to the Royal Opera House, while the Kentish Opera Group received by contrast £100, twenty-five pounds more than Tunbridge Wells Opera at £75.

In spite of its greatly increased size, however, there was a distinct muffling of the Council's tone. Some of the old headmasterly arrogance had disappeared with maturity, and in its place there is a defensiveness, a tone of wary apology, that reminds one less of a Public School Common Room than of the Secret Service. The Twenty-Ninth Arts Council Report (1973–4) is quite extraordinarily nervous, high-pitched, even a little hysterical, as if the populism of Jennie Lee's White Paper, the demands of youth that the White Paper encouraged, and the pressures of a new Minister for the Arts who wanted to make the Arts Council more "democratic" were all too much for its ageing frame. The doings of the young Arts Council read something like one of P. G. Wodehouse's school stories. A narrative of the middle-aged Arts Council reads more like an improbable novel jointly written by Angela Brazil and John le Carré.

The Council was of course caught in an economic trap. It had taken on "new" arts ventures over the previous five years, and now, with a sharp increase in inflation, it was finding even its increased resources were insufficient to meet its obligations. The triennial funding urged by the White Paper and introduced two years before had been abandoned before the end of the first triennium. It was moreover on the end of another painful political fork. The February election of 1974 brought Hugh Jenkins to the Arts Minister's office. Mr Jenkins knew the Arts Council well, having served on it from 1967 to 1971, and he brought with him a desire to see it actually change in accordance with the White Paper, which its members had so enthusiastically received. He also carried a further threat. He wanted the members of the Arts Council, its four panels and three

major committees, to be elected by the various interested parties; in his
own terms, he announced that he wanted the Council to be more "democratic".

The Report is wearily defensive of the Council's existence and offers a
string of apologies and convoluted explanations. Some of the latter are
very odd indeed:

> As it is, the Council has in its Panels and Committees the benefit of
> a wide range of skills and experience, managerial, financial and
> critical as well as artistic. Their members should differ in artistic
> outlook and in age (each Panel has many members under thirty-
> five) and they must bring knowledge of different parts of the
> country. It is difficult to see how all this specialist advice could be
> obtained, unless Panel members were invited to serve by the Coun-
> cil itself.... .

The difficulty of seeing surely holds only within the Arts Council. Some
of these members, however, boldly—and, perhaps, unwisely—outlined
the powers of the Arts Council's bureaucrats: "It is, however, the role of
the staff in the making of grants that is sometimes questioned. Of course
officers 'process' the applications. Council Panels and Committees could
not otherwise make their judgements." And of course it must not be
thought that there is a free critical dialogue going on within the Council:
"Council officers, from the moment they join the staff, learn that they
have to temper their own judgement and artistic tastes to a 'Council
view'...." Much of the report, however, concentrates on showing that
the Arts Council's actions are justified because it is often criticized from
opposite points of view. This is a favourite Arts Council theme, offered
as proof that the Council is somewhere "in the middle" and hence more
or less right about everything:

> To many individual creative artists, it seems that the Council
> responds too readily to energetic efforts of promoters of expensive
> schemes for the arts involving performance, while ignoring the
> claims of the writer, the composer and the artist.
>
> Those, on the other hand, responsible for the operation of hun-
> dreds of enterprises in theatre, music, opera and ballet, think that
> the Council spreads its resources too thinly by adding others to
> their number, or by embarking on a multitude of schemes for the
> benefit of artists and writers who can, at any rate, find some market
> for their work, however limited or unrewarding that market
> may be.... .
>
> The emergent companies and experimental groups think that too
> much goes to the middle-class establishment.

In picturing itself as being caught in crossfire, the Council is not of course claiming that it is trying to mediate between different schools of criticism, or that it is in some way searching for a true national balance between all the arts. It is merely saying that it is under attack from a number of pressure groups—hence the forlorn pleas that all its Panels have somebody under 35 on them, and also contain provincial persons who can tell the Arts Council what it's like outside London. The Secretary-General of the time, Sir Hugh Willatt, is defending the Arts Council because in the face of attacks from different places it makes expedient political accommodations, not because it makes good artistic judgements.

He continues to talk of the Arts Council and its subsidized chicks as if they are the entirety of "the arts", and for all problems, political, economic or cultural, he continues to offer the same well-worn panacea: "There is point in all this criticism. The deficiencies revealed are genuine enough. An increase in Council funds would go a long way to provide the remedy."

Which brings us to a further characteristic of the Arts Council's behaviour. Throughout its mature years, and as it slid into decline, it would constantly wheedle like an old tramp that a little more money, just a little more, would solve everything. It could not ask for less, or for a lot more, without acknowledging that its choice of clients had been wrong, and its definition of "art" simply trimmed to fit its frame. It was always some external circumstance—inflation, taxes, the increased price of wood[2]—which was causing the problem, never the misjudgements of the Council itself.

In 1956 the Arts Council Secretary had written:

> Two and a half million a year would adequately finance not only the range of enterprises which the Arts Council and the Local Authorities assist—and which, because of wage increases, will cost much more next year than this—but would also provide the money for the long-term rehousing of the arts... it should be multiplied by at least 2½ if, in the next ten years, something substantial and permanent is to be built on the basis of the last ten years.

In fact the government grant of 1956 (£820,000) was multiplied by considerably more than that over the succeeding decade, even allowing for inflation. By 1966 it had risen to £3,910,000, and in 1967—the year in which the recommendations of the White Paper took effect—it rose to £5,700,000, and had thus multiplied in numerical terms by nearly seven. Nevertheless, six years after that, and with the grant (in plain numerical terms) once more trebled, and running at £17,138,000, the Secretary

General was still suggesting that "an increase in funds" would go a long way towards solving the Arts Council's problems.

In the following year's report, at the conclusion of what were his seven years in office, Sir Hugh Willatt produced a lengthy account of where the great increase in government grant aid to the Council had gone. He argued that in that period the "jewels in the crown", the four big national organizations, had in fact seen their grant aid expand more slowly than that of the Arts Councils of Scotland and Wales, the Regional Arts Associations, and touring schemes. Other areas of real growth had included Dance and Opera, Arts Centres and "Regional Projects", "Community Arts"[3] and Literature. Literature had indeed risen from £63,000 in 1967–8 to almost £200,000 in 1974–5. (It is perhaps rather snide to point out that in both years grant aid to Literature represents roughly one fifth of the Council's own operating costs, and that even here the trend was towards assisting organizations rather than artists: grants to individual writers—less than a fifth of the total sum paid to Arts Council secretaries—rose from £43,000 to £55,000, while that paid to the publishers of magazines rose in the period from £8,000 to £34,000.)

There are faint hints in the Report which warn us of the coming of the money-fixated 1980s:

> There is of course a return from tourism. Travel advertisements in a number of countries say, "Come to Britain for its arts and entertainment"; to London, to Edinburgh, Stratford on Avon, Aldeburgh, Chichester and a dozen more places where a theatre, an orchestra or a festival are a tourist magnet. There is the return in the form of foreign currency, resulting from the visits of British companies and orchestras, singers and instrumentalists abroad.

There is more than a hint, too, of the desirability of "private patronage" supplementing state aid. "The Royal Opera House," notes the Report, "has in recent years raised substantial money from private sources." But the main theme is, as ever, Give us just a *little* bit more:

> Council reports and public statements have had, lately, to strike a gloomy, even a desperate note, calling attention to the fragile financial situation of so many of its clients. This note must again be struck. Inflation has hit our clients very hard. They are "labour intensive" and the cost of materials they use has multiplied many times.

This particular sort of special pleading is dealt with elsewhere, but whatever kinds of economic ailments are fashionably supposed to afflict the arts, the remedy—a modest increase in state funds—is always the same.

And the Arts Council's grant, in spite of all its intermittent increases over the years, has stayed at more or less the same proportionate level (relative to public spending) since its size was hastily determined in the first summer of its life. The government grant in the Council's first full year of operation—£235,000—was about one eight hundredth of what the public spent on all kinds of leisure activities in that year. (They spent £97,000,000 on gambling, which was their chief pleasure in 1946, and £50,000,000 on going to the cinema, the next most expensive activity.) The figures still run very roughly in that kind of proportion: the Arts Council funds remain a small proportion of the public's spending on leisure—always less than 0·25%. (Indeed, although one does not suggest any sinister relationship, the Arts Council's government grant has always been about the same as the amount that is stolen by shoplifters each year in the centre of London.[4])

The political reasons for the annual public posturing over the size of the Arts Council's grant are obvious enough. It is clear how its general size was politically determined in the first place. It is also obvious that it would always be impolitic for the Council as constituted to ask for more than a little increase each year. And Ministers for the Arts plainly "hold" the Arts Council's grant down one year, demonstrating the requisite toughness to their colleagues, then "fight for" an increase "ahead of inflation" in another year, thus demonstrating the government's deep concern for cultural values, and pleasing the subsidized "arts" world. The politics of it all could not be clearer. What is damaging is dressing it all up as if it is done out of a concern for Art, with political enconomics the higher reality that must be acknowledged and won over before Art's faery kingdom can be given any substance. The damaging pretence was that the system placed the Arts Council "on the side of the arts", against politicians, whereas it was in reality part of a knot of conspiracy tied by politicians. If not actually hostile to the arts, the Council's bureaucracy too often exhausted the organizations it supported and, by recognizing excellence only when political parameters widened to allow it, the Council became parasitic upon the country's artists.

Thus, as the Arts Council moved stealthily from being a responsive body to acting as if it were actually responsible for the state of the national culture, it canonized as "art" each year just enough activities to use up its funds. The size of the government grant thus determined each year in advance just how much excellent drama, how much excellent painting and how much excellent music there would be. As the size of the Arts Council's grant was, from the first, politically determined, so, by the Arts Council's definition, was the amount of excellence in art each year likewise politically determined. The resulting political accommoda-

tions, financial balances and managerial systems meshed with the carefully fostered illusion of critical detachment. This meant that both
Council and clients were chronically stifled. And although efforts were
made in succeeding years to breathe vigorous life back into the faltering
body, the Arts Council was doomed to grow old gracelessly.

5

Sickness and the Knife

From the appointment of Roy Shaw as the Arts Council's Secretary General in 1975 the Council seemed gradually to take on even more of the colour of the secret services. There was the secrecy, of course, and the infuriating assurance that as the Council's officers were somehow "on the inside" of the arts, all criticism of their actions was ill-informed and provincial. The Council even mirrored MI5 by developing a series of warring cells within its workforce, investigating "leaks" of its own classified information, and searching for "moles" within its own divided ranks.

The publication of the Literature Director's Autobiography[1] made public what was known by some at the time, that Shaw did not get on with many of his Directors and was, for periods of his tenure, in a state of siege. There were other fraternal feuds, relationships with the working arts world became fractious, and accusations of duplicity became commonplace. The tension within the Council was such that, at an Arts Council conference at Stratford-on-Avon in May, 1978, a recommendation was made to carry out a review of the way in which the Council worked.[2]

A Working Party, comprising the Lord Hutchinson, Q.C., Mr John Manduell, Mr Howard Newby, and the Hon. John Sainsbury was appointed, and began its work in September of that year. It took much evidence from the Council's own staff, and examined its bureaucratic structure in some detail. It recognized the tension within the organization readily enough: "We have become aware through a great deal of the evidence submitted to us of a widespread sense of malaise and a low level of morale among many of the staff." And, as was perhaps inevitable in an Arts Council report, the Working Party suggested that it was partly the government's fault for not giving them the annual increases they had asked for: "No doubt one cause of this is the frustration which a period of no growth has inevitably imposed after a decade of rapid expansion in the arts." (They meant, after a decade of rapid expansion of arts subsidy.) The other suggested reasons for the general malaise were the familiar excuses for bureaucratic failings everywhere:

But we believe that the poor morale is more significantly attributa-
ble to the problems of pay and grading, inadequacies of the management structure and of communication and a lack of an agreed
and understood policy accompanied by firm direction from the top.

Nothing then to do with art, the condition of artists, with the government and the Arts Council's willingness to make use of "the arts" as
diplomatic and economic counters, or with the state of the national culture? Just a matter of paying the officers more and getting "an agreed and
understood policy", and "firm direction from the top".

The last, fatal, spasm of the Arts Council's life, when it became
obsessed, above all else, with its own management, is presaged by this
scantily noticed Report.[3] It contains within it all the germs of the Council's later capitulation to the twin gods of Management and Mammon.
For the moment, however, the Arts Council had more immediate problems.

                              *   *   *

From its earliest days the Arts Council had described its activities in
gardening metaphors. The obvious conflict between supporting the best
in the arts and distributing art equally over the country, a conflict which
had been at the heart of the Council's deepening confusions, had been
smeared over by a classically bland phrase, "Raise and spread!" But in
the early eighties, as the Council's problems reached crisis point, no
horticultural tag could divert attention from its dilemma.

The total government grant to the Arts Council had risen from
£51,800,000 in 1978–9 to £63,125,000 in 1979–80, and had risen again to
£70,970,000 in 1980–81. What appeared to be an even larger grant increase was obtained by the Minister for the Arts, Norman St John Stevas,
in 1981–2, when the total rose to £80,250,000. In those years, however,
the amounts available to clients rose very little. Partly this was because
chunks of the Council's apparent increases were "marked" for new and
favoured large-scale clients—£1,000,000 of new money had to be found
between 1978 and 1980 for the English National Opera North at Leeds,
new money had to be found to finance the National Theatre's move from
the Old Vic to the South Bank in 1976, and a further £500,000 for the
new theatres which had opened (partly as a result of receiving "Housing
the Arts" grants) at Bromley, Ipswich, Salisbury and Manchester. Partly
too revenue funding remained static because inflation was said by the arts
bureaucracy to have eroded the value of the government's grants to the
Arts Council—even those that seemed to have increased by a good deal
more than the inflation rate.

The "effects of inflation" in the arts had become a talking point in the political / arts world both in Britain and in the United States. The argument was usually based upon the notion that the arts, all of them, were themselves sufficiently similar, but sufficiently unlike everything else, to have discrete economic trends which could be tabulated and presented to governments (as "proof" that the arts required ever-expanding subsidy). Following the early work by the American economist William Baumol (1964), the "inevitable" arts hyper-inflation—caused, apparently, by the "inevitable" labour-intensiveness of all the arts—was usually termed "Bohmol's disease", and was used by non-economists (that is, managers, bureaucrats and arts politicians) as if it signified some generally applicable law. The phrase was widely used to wheedle extra money from governments for the use of arts bureaucrats.

Yet a close reading of the work in question[4] reveals that "Baumol's disease" was a journalistic phrase which had been crudely hacked from its proper academic moorings. As an alarmed Baumol wrote in 1985:

> Since the cost disease was described in 1964, arts administrators throughout the world have been using the model to back up their requests for increases in government support for the arts. It has repeatedly been argued that since performance budgets must inevitably rise faster than the general price level, increases in support which merely match the economy's price level must condemn the arts to decline and deterioration.... .
>
> First, as we have seen, the cost disease is a manifestation of the *relative* lag in productivity growth. Performance suffers because manufacturing productivity habitually rises too rapidly and pulls wages up with it. But in the 1970s, for reasons that are in some dispute, productivity growth in almost every nationalized economy slowed to a crawl. Thus the engine that triggers the cost disease virtually ran out of fuel during that decade.
>
> Second, even the earliest study of the cost disease of the arts indicated that while for well over a century orchestral cost per performance had *almost* always risen faster than the general price level, there was one persistent exception—periods of inflation.[5]

There were thus three good reasons, all well known to academics in Arts Management, why the so-called "cost disease" did not automatically apply to "the arts" in all circumstances. First, the only reliable work on it had been done in the U.S., and on orchestras (which have, obviously, utterly different economic characteristics from, say, potter's workshops, or small publishers, or travelling circuses). Second, as productivity growth both in the U.S. and Britain had slowed throughout the 1970s one major condition of "cost disease" no longer held. Thirdly, and perhaps most crucially, it had specifically been shown that "cost disease" did not occur in times of high inflation.

None of this seemed to trouble the Arts Council's Secretary General, Roy Shaw, who announced in the 36th Arts Council Report, for 1980–1 that the figure for "inflation in the arts" *was*—no argument brooked—higher than general inflation,[6] and added that the Council had commissioned "independent research" to determine "how much higher".[7]

But by then "commissioning research" was of no more use than the sudden discovery of some untarnished garden metaphor would have been. The Arts Council itself was in financial crisis, having done what it had warned its clients never to do—overextended its own financial commitments. After much examination of its own bureaucratic entrails the Council decided, in December 1980, that it would "axe" 41 of its clients. It used the money thus "saved" to give substantially increased grant aid to 46 other clients while the remaining thousand or so received a more or less standard increase.

The spur to make these changes was economic: the Arts Council argued that the government hadn't given them as much extra as they wished. Until the crisis the Council had stedfastly maintained that it supported only "the best", and that all its clients had been supported for good artistic reasons. Yet the decision to cut state subsidy from forty-one hitherto of "the best" was presented by Shaw not as an economic accommodation, still less as an admission of past economic foolishness by the Council, but as a *critical* judgement. "The Arts Council," he insisted, "is in the business of making critical judgements." *Critical Judgements* was the title he gave to the 1980–1 Annual Report, in which he defended the Council's actions. The conclusion could only be that in previous years the Arts Council had *not* been making critical judgements, but that now a new and astringent intelligence was rectifying the situation.

Yet that report suggests that decisions were taken on almost every basis *except* that of critical judgement. First, Shaw is anxious to say that the Arts Council has made its decisions as a demonstration of its virility:

> Sir Hugh Willatt, my predecessor as Secretary-General, noted in a book recently published... that we were moving into "less happy times" and suggested that this would certainly impose on the Arts Council "the need to make choices which, hitherto, to the great benefit of the arts, they have been able to avoid." Opinions differ about whether it was in fact good for the Council to avoid making tough decisions: in November 1980 the *Guardian*'s arts reporter wrote scathingly that the Council had "neither spunk nor daring" to cut out clients. He was wrong. In December, the Council showed that it had both.

Note how Willatt's "choices" become "tough decisions", and how Shaw relishes the journalist's equation of cutting clients with showing "spunk and daring". See how we are allowed to infer that it is good for the Council to feel the smack of firm government, and face up to what it had for too long avoided–the need to get tough with artists. Overall the language of the Secretary General's Report is that of a politician rather than a critic, and of a politician who readily drops into the prescriptive tones of the social scientist:

> The need to preserve a balance of provision between London and the other regions explains a number of the Council's decisions. It is the reason, for example, why the Council warned the Prospect (touring) Theatre Company when it moved four years ago into the Old Vic that the Arts Council could in no way fund what spokesmen for the company described to us as "a third national theatre company" in London.

From there Shaw drops into the jargon of the economist, saying that *box-office returns* were in some cases the major criterion, and in others that clients had to qualify for Arts Council support by their success in *raising local authority money*. Amongst other criteria were, first, that clients must be *full-time professionals* (the Council had until that time funded three national amateur organizations) and second, that they must be *efficient in their use of available resources*.

There are two passing mentions of "artistic quality" but nothing to give the reader confidence that such an organization, working in secret, and proclaiming so many, inevitably conflicting, criteria as the basis of its decisions, could be relied upon to recognize quality in art. It would seem that the Council created bureaucratic strategies (the need to "preserve a balance of provision between London and the other regions", for example), and that it had reasssuringly solid notions of what constituted managerial efficiency, but that it then fitted applicants into their predetermined slots (suppose that the Prospect Theatre Company had in fact, managerially and artistically, been *very much* better than any comparable group in any other region?) It is surely reasonable to say that when terms from production-line management are used—like *efficiency*—then the primary judgement being made is not of artistic quality. A better title for that report would have been *Managerial Judgements*.

As it staggered through its own mid-life crisis, the beleaguered Council chose to label all criticism of its actions as ill-motivated hostility to the arts:

> Critics of the Arts Council... are often drawn from ex-clients or would-be clients with a sense of grievance (we have to reject

hundreds of new applications each year) or from the ranks of
philistines of all kinds.[8]

"Critics of the Council" were thus assumed to have squalid motives and
not to be worth arguing with. ED Berman, the then director of Inter-
Action, staged a series of public "trials" of the Arts Council on the stage
of the Tricycle Theatre. (It included witnesses such as the Sheffield
researcher who had been commissioned by the Arts Council to investigate whether members of its Literature Panel had been distributing too
many grants to their friends. He found they had, and the Arts Council
promptly suppressed his report.) Shaw's reaction to the "trial" was to
ban his officers from attending or from taking part, presumably because
participants and audience at the North London theatre were all nursing
grievances or were irredeemably philistine.)

The Council was so seized with its own "toughness" that it could not
demean itself by taking part in pubic debate.[9] Yet the widespread hostility to the Arts Council was no longer that of the forties and early fifties,
when anything "arty" from the Third Programme, the well-established
British Council or the new Arts Council was pilloried by the press. The
criticism now came from artists, from critics, from concerned academics
who disliked the Council's belligerent assumption of superiority, disliked
the ways in which it had taken over respectable critical language for its
own purposes and disliked above all its refusal to be accountable in the
way a critic must always be accountable—by engaging in creative argument.

It remained perfectly possible to support the idea of state support for
the arts, but also to see that the Arts Council was not a good channel for
distributing state money. For the Council had begun to interpret the
"arm's length principle" as a mandate for it to act in secret, and for
almost everybody else (bull-necked party politicians, unsubsidized pari-
ahs, and the common philistines) to be excluded from their world. What
had been intended as a convention to keep party politics out of making
critical judgements in the arts had become a charter for another kind of
political domination of them.

*   *   *

The relationship between each Minister for the Arts, each Chairman of
the Arts Council and each Secretary General varies markedly. At the time
of the 1980–1 "cuts" it was plain that the Minister, Norman St John
Stevas, and the Secretary General, (now) Sir Roy Shaw, disagreed
violently. Upon his retirement Shaw attacked not only Stevas, but two

other ministers. Stevas later replied in a letter to *The Guardian* (23 July, 1983):

> He boasts that having left his paid public office, he threw aside his mask of impartiality and attacked myself and two of my predecessors. I should have thought a decent reticence about such dubious behaviour would have been more appropriate. I am however not surprised by this action. While I had the happiest relationship with Sir Kenneth Robinson, then Chairman of the Arts Council, I found that Sir Roy represented a temperamental incompatibility. I understand that Sir William Rees-Mogg, Chairman of the Arts Council, found the same difficulty.

Stevas accused Sir Roy of attempting to blame him and the government for the cuts, and said that "the way these cuts were communicated was disgraceful." (Earlier, when Stevas had himself been sacked by Mrs Thatcher, he had thrown aside his own mask of impartiality and said that the Council under Shaw looked like a "star chamber operation" which had used methods that were "ill-judged and incompatible with civilized values".)

In one sense these abusive rallies pointed up what was supposed to be a cornerstone of the "British system". For the relationship between the elected politicians (in particular the Minister for the Arts). and the Council (and its officers), was supposed to be governed by the much-venerated "arm's length principle". The Redcliffe Maud Report on the Arts (1976) had laid much stress on this, and Shaw certainly did. The essential point about the "principle" was that it supposedly inhibits *elected* politicians from playing any part in the making of critical judgements, thus preventing any "party politics" from interfering in the way taxpayers' money is spent. The advantage to Arts Ministers was that it meant they didn't have to answer questions about art in the House of Commons (they always were able to reply "That is a matter for the Arts Council") and the advantage to artists was supposed to be that party politicians did not interfere in the making of judgements which were artistic, and not political.

If indeed the Council had been composed of persons competent to make artistic judgements and if their decisions *had* been critical decisions, without political taint, then Shaw's vehement defence of the "principle" would have had much to commend it. One could have defended the exclusion of all politicians from the Council's deliberations on the simple grounds that the Council manifestly could do what had to be done better without them.

But that was not the case. The Arts Council now consisted of almost

anybody except genuine art critics—of politicians, industrialists, economists, developers, local councillors, solicitors and other such admirables.
Those members of the Arts Council were, moreover, appointed (then as
now) by the government minister.[10] So, whether or not they happened to
have some real interest in the arts or happened to have some genuine
critical ability (some had) the fact remains that they were all appointed by
politicians for political reasons. And they were advised by the Arts Council's officers, who were effectively civil servants, who had, in Sir Hugh
Willatt's phrase (above) to temper their own judgement to a "Council
view".

The Council arrives at its decisions without engaging in public debate.
There is no creative argument between the Council and the artists,
between Council and public, or (on occasions such as the 1980–1 "cuts")
between the Council and the Minister. The Arts Council is *financially*
accountable—a mercy when it is realized that if its grant from government
had continued to increase at the rate it did during Norman St John
Stevas's period as Minister, the Council would shortly after the millennium be spending a *billion* pounds of taxpayers' money—but *it is not
accountable for its critical judgements*. So when the Arts Council, in the
fashionable managerial argot of the eighties, spoke of giving "value for
money" to government, it meant that governments had to be told that
"the arts" had a high economic, or political value. Nothing compelled
the Council to argue to government for the aesthetic and spiritual values
of art, and, as it would not engage in critical debates with artists or
public, its central purposes were carried out in secret, and it was a public
body, paid for from taxes, whose major function was beyond accountability.

This left the Council free to talk with apparent authority, in its utterances that were so clearly given out for political eyes, about the politics or
economics of the arts. So, in the early eighties, they duly began to
assert—as unchallengeable fact—that "the arts" played a great role in
what was becoming the highest national purpose, wealth creation. Shaw,
sometimes dexterous in political argument, and capable of making
luminous distinctions in the language of arts administration (between
"accessibility" and "availability" for example) seemed to take economics on trust from his advisers, and left some terrible hostages to post-
erity: "A point which is often overlooked is that the arts (unlike say,
health or education) actually earn money for the country, especially from
the tourist trade."

Even ignoring the by now habitual gathering of every kind of creative
activity into one plastic bag, "the arts", this was a most unfortunate
caveat. The terms are of dissimilar kinds; health and education may be

compared with "art", which of itself does nothing to earn money, but the activities and constructs signified by Shaw's Arts Council usage of *the arts* have an economic dimension. It would be fairer to compare "the arts" with professional sport, which is profitable business, or with universities, which plainly *do* earn us quite a lot of foreign cash.

Saying even that "the arts" earn "especially from the tourist trade" is more disingenuous, particularly when it is used as an argument to justify state subsidy. There is no evidence that the subsidized arts are any kind of major attraction to Britain's incoming tourists—the PSI *The Economic Importance of the Arts in Britain* (1988) reported that only 7% of overseas arts tourists [*sic*] to Britain gave the arts as their sole reason for visiting Britain, and, if no arts attractions had been available to them, only 5% of them would have cancelled their trip! (Tables 4.13, 4.14) The survey gives no indication of the attitudes of tourists in general, but the figures for tourist spending would suggest that the arts earn far less money from tourists than from almost any other kind of recreational amusement, or from selling plain junk.

In particular, the claim that they earn money from tourism is a poor argument for increased government aid for the arts. One effect of subsidy is to keep prices low for well-to-do arts patrons. Government figures now show that the AB social classes—from which audiences at the best subsidized salons are predominantly drawn—now take three or more overseas holidays a year, contributing considerably to Britain's "tourist deficit", which has steadily expanded since Shaw made his remark, and now stands at more than two billion pounds a year. It could be argued therefore that the subsidy system indirectly contributes to the country's *losing* from tourism. For the better-off are left with more money to spend abroad. In 1990 Sir Alfred Sherman put the point cogently:

> A minority of theatres, whose ideology, excessive labour costs or standards of acting and choice of plays makes them uncompetitive, demand subsidies, brandishing the argument that theatres deserve subsidies because they attract tourists. What proportion of package and back-pack tourists have the cultural background, the money or the taste to benefit from theatre in general and subsidized theatre in particular is never disclosed. With the bland circular reasoning characteristic of our masters, tourism's "minders" justify subsidies with the unsupported and unquantified argument that tourists patronize theatres.
>
> The government should be obliged to institute objective and honest cost-benefit studies of tourist-promotion, to include environmental costs and dis-benefits; it might well show that tourist promotion costs this country more than it earns.

It may well be, Sherman suggests, that some tourism should be taxed, not subsidized. The Arts Council's abject hitching of "the arts" to the gravy train of "tourism" throughout the eighties certainly pointed up a confusion. The appeal for more state subsidy—just a *little* more each year—had been based upon the "truth" that the best in art could not, for one reason or another, support itself in the open market. Now Shaw (and his successors) started to talk of the arts as if they were part of an economic process, and a process that was ultimately profitable. There was, it seemed, no difference—no economic difference, that is—between "the arts" and the tourist junk sold in hotel foyers. So money going to arts enterprises was no longer a form of charitable donation, but "venture capital", state subsidy was "investment" and successful artists were distinguished from the others not by virtue of their artistic quality, but by virtue of their economic "enterprise".

One does not, of course, have to be an enemy of the Council to see that this line of argument is likely to become tangled, and likely to lead politicians and public to become much more sceptical of state subsidy. If "the arts" are to be defined as a part of an ultimately profitable, wealth-creating economic process, then why should they not be—in the jargon of the day—"privatized"? If "the arts" were what Shaw's successor as Secretary General bullishly claimed—"a successful part of Great Britain Plc"—then why should shares in British Art not be as popular as those in British Gas? Tell Sid, it's Carl André.

*   *   *

In the early eighties, however, the bandwagon of "Business Sponsorship" once more began to roll. In his time as Minister, Norman St John Stevas produced an expensive-looking pamphlet purporting to tell arts organizations how to go about getting "business sponsorship". Successive Ministers leaned upon the Council in order to make it adopt American schemes for joint public and private "funding" of "the arts". It was soon being noised abroad that state support of the arts had reached a plateau, and that from now on deficits would have to be made good by private money. Then followed a propaganda wave—described further in a comment upon Sir William Rees-Mogg below—to say that this expensive attitudinizing had all been a great success, that arts organizations in Britain had been forced by it to face up to "reality" (*reality* being, in this case, the practices of American corporations). Moreover, we were assured by such a disinterested voice as that of the Association for Business Sponsorship in the Arts, that "business sponsorship" in Britain had triumphantly risen in the eighties from "next to nothing" to some "thirty million pounds a year".

The entire campaign was a political stunt. The majority of arts organizations in Britain had never, as successive Ministers announced they had, been wholly reliant upon state monies. Only a minority had been supported by Arts Council subsidies at all, and even they did not fall into one standard economic pattern. The greater number of arts activities in Britain had never been *dependent* upon state aid, but had been sustained by a great variety of other economic means, including, in its various guises, *at least 150 years of support from the private sector.*

For this was the second flaw in the picture Ministers tried to present. They spoke of "business sponsorship" as if the Americans had recently invented it, as if it was a new idea for the eighties. The truth is that in the nineteenth century industrialists had built Britain's theatres and concert halls, commissioned its artists, and subsidized the cultural lives of its workforce to a far greater degree than anyone was doing in the mid-twentieth century. It is therefore nonsense to say that "business sponsorship" in Britain rose from "next to nothing". By any reasonable account, private-sector support of the arts in Britain has been in irregular but steep *decline* over the past century.

That private support of the arts had by the end of the eighties "risen" to some thirty million pounds a year—a figure repeated so often by Arts Council propagandists that serious newspapers took to printing it as fact—can readily be disproved. Indeed, it can only be sustained for a moment by adopting the well-worn Arts Council parameters—that is, by looking only at Arts Council clients, as if they constitute the entirety of "the arts". Beyond these narrow confines many arts organizations had no need of the miraculous new "business sponsorship". For example, in that same period, Britain's ten largest publishers were actually making combined annual *profits* of more than thirty million, and Britain's commercial music industry was making profits ten times greater than that. Other segments of the "arts industry" which *were* in need of "new money", however, seemed to see very little of this supposed increase in sponsorship. The British film industry, for example, between 1984–5 and 1988–9 suffered a *decrease* in private investment of some *eighty* million pounds.

Successive Arts Ministers continued nevertheless to mouth the political platitudes about the need for the "growing demand" for the arts to be funded equally by private and public money, but their actions showed clearly enough that they did not believe what they were saying. The government's own financial allocation to "the arts" continued to rise, sometimes spectacularly, throughout the eighties. (In the Conservative Party's first decade of government from 1979 the government's annual grant to the Arts Council rose by 48% in real terms.)

Ministers seemed to turn a blind eye however to the fact that large
parts of the swelling state grant paid for a new kind of consultant and arts
bureaucrat—the Fund Raising Officer. These were plainly political
appointments. For the most part their function was to display conspicu-
ous virtue by well-publicized "approaches" to the private sector for
money, and in filling in Arts Council applications saying that they had
done this. Very few raised enough new money to pay their salaries, and
bizarrely the government in effect financed a new clutch of state bureaucrats, whose duty it was to extol the virtues of being supported by private
money. It is a reasonable estimate that, even if "business sponsorship" in
Britain *had* "risen" to anything like £30,000,000, it would not have paid
for the new bureaucratic machine called into being to propagandize about
its virtues.

6

Towards the Other World

In 1983, under the chairmanship of Sir William Rees-Mogg, the Arts Council announced (rather oddly, in view of all the bitterness and turmoil that had gone before) that it was "stuck in a groove", and that it was going, once more, to undertake a thorough and fundamental review of itself. It had been "spreading its resources too widely and hence too thinly, at the expense of vital, primary aspects of its work". From now on it was going to be the main "power house" of the arts, be more interventionist, and was going to move towards the "real world". So, after much ponderous puffing, six months of bureaucratic banter, a strange "Arts Council weekend" held at Ilkley, and the expenditure (so it was said) of £7,000, the Council brought forth a 44-page pamphlet entitled *The Glory of the Garden* [sic]. This, it announced, was "a strategy for a decade", although it was not clear whether the pamphlet was intended to be a manual for the use of the subsidy officers and their clients, or whether it had more ambitious aims, and sought to offer a grand ten-year blueprint for the whole of British culture. For whether the pamphlet thought it was addressing the state funding bureaucracy, the much wider "arts world" or the general cultural condition of the nation, was never very clear:

> There have been important changes in the nature of the society which the Council seeks to serve through its spending on the arts. The growth of enforced leisure, the severe economic depression of many of our older city centres, changing perceptions of the requirements of a multicultural society and the rapid development of new communications media all have implications for the arts and for those charged with funding the arts.

Those implications apparently included a necessity to undertake a special kind of survey. The Council did not propose to investigate the supply of art, nor, that time, did it intend to investigate "demand". (That, as ever, was simply presumed to be increasing, all the time, everywhere.) Instead it said it was looking at something which could apparently be quantified more readily, a new curiosity which had been worming its way up

through the Arts Council dictionary for some years, an entity called
"provision", neither supply nor demand:

> It is proper that the Council's attention should be directed in the
> first place to the provision of the arts across the country, that it
> should seek to help to rectify gaps in that provision, and to
> improve the standards of existing provision, before turning to the
> implications of such changes for its own functions and internal
> methods of operation.

What is *provision* in the arts? What were the "standards of provision" in
eighteenth-century Lichfield, say, or nineteenth-century Nottingham,
and how might an Arts Council of that time have gone about "improv-
ing" them? Who, other than the customers, actually sets the right level of
"provision" which each area should enjoy, from each art? Is "provision" of art still the same when no good art is being produced? Is there
such a thing as "provision" of the unsubsidized arts? None of these
questions does *The Glory of the Garden* address. However, reading the
pamphlet makes it clear that whatever a gap in the "provision" of art
may be, it can be cured by the application of another Arts Council entity,
"development". Rees-Mogg's Arts Council uses both words a lot:

> The ideal possibility is this: an area with a large potential audience,
> still under-served in the provision of a particular art; a local
> authority or authorities keen to work with the Arts Council or the
> Regional Arts Associations on developing the arts to the highest
> possible standard; local private initiatives through administration
> and sponsorship to help finance the development; a core of talent of
> high quality wanting to carry the work forward. These are ideal
> conditions, not always realizable. . . .

One keeps sliding through such stuff, feeling the nose harden and the
muscles flex, but unfortunately feeling at the same moment that the
brain is turning to slime. What *is* Rees-Mogg talking about? In these
"ideal" circumstances, the dreaded "under-serving" having been noted,
"keenness" having been shown, and "initiatives" prepared to "develop" from "a core of talent of high quality", *what is actually going to
happen*? Is a neglected author going to be published? Is good new music
going to be performed? Or—the brain begins to liquidize again—is it that
existing "provision" of existing state-subsidized art is going to be somehow levelled up? Are people going to be compulsorily trained in the
enjoyment of something they have hitherto not had much time
for?—Jackson Pollock's painting? Cage's music? Peter Porter's poetry?
Reggae in the cowsheds and maypole dancing in the inner cities? It is

obvious that under-serving + development = proper provision, but *of what*?

Well, "the Arts", that's of what. A new kind of "Art" in which economic value and spiritual value are assumed to be the same. For Rees-Mogg "the Arts" are an undifferentiated economic substance, owned by the metropolitan cultural bureaucrats and nothing much to do with artists. For we have now reached the point at which artists are sometimes horrified by "the Arts", by "the overpaid, unnecessary mercenaries of subsidy". The playwright John Osborne developed his antagonism in an article in *The Observer* (10 June 1986):

> I have worked in my profession for almost forty years. During the first half of that time I was amazingly blessed. The life, the endeavour, the people who shared my good fortune, the revel and risk of our chosen game has gone. To you, unstricken by the flawed adventure of us reckless living players and Gypsies, it may be about something now called "The Arts" ....
>
> Consider the people who are in charge of it all, the time-serving nonentities who, in their unflagging pushiness, get themselves entrenched as chairmen, governors, committee stooges and opinionated show-offs, the members of the boards of hospitals, opera houses, newspapers, and, most destructively, of theatres.
>
> Consider them; these self-appointed traffic-wardens of culture—the deadly "Arts"—as if the most profound and mysterious of human endeavours were as identifiable and open to purchase as items on a market stall.

For Rees-Mogg "the Arts" is a coagulated substance with mysterious healing properties, for which we have both a demand and a need:

> The arts, human, creative, inspiring, individual, warm, alive, provide a natural healing to this sense of depersonalization, and the appreciation of beauty can transcend the moon-like chill of an electronic world.... Perhaps we demand the arts more than earlier generations: perhaps we need the arts more than earlier generations.
>
> Whatever the reasons, the demand is a fact....

And these proven "demands" apparently "justify a significant, if thrifty, public expenditure."

At this point the mist clears a little. It would appear that the words "provision" and "development" are eonomic terms like all the rest. The words refer to practices in public expenditure, in the way the Arts Councils and the R.A.A.s spend our taxes. "Provision" refers to an amount of subsidy given to the arts in an area. An area is deemed to be "under-served" in an art form when that art draws less subsidy than in other equivalent areas. "Development" is bringing the area up to scratch by topping up its levels of public subsidy (and employing more state bureaucrats to administer it, write reports on it and so on) so that it is, in bureaucratic terms, exactly the same as everywhere else.

As for the "demand", the demand which is just "a fact", it would appear not to be an ordinary old-fashioned kind of demand at all. If people in an area really do demand, say, organ music, then they will organize organ recitals and buy tickets for them, the price and sale of which cover costs. That is a well-understood arrangement which has been going on for centuries. It enables us to say that there was a huge demand for organ music recitals in the eighteenth century, or for drama in the nineteenth century, or for Dickens's novels or Reynolds's painting. But Rees-Mogg's kind of demand isn't like that. His demand *justifies subsidy*. The demand which is a fact is the swelling demand for more state aid.

It is of course possible to conceive of a genuine public demanding an art—opera, say—who could not afford to stage or to buy commercially-priced tickets for it without subvention from some other source. And it is also possible to have a group of people who demand art but haven't got the ability to organize it for themselves or haven't got the money—young children, say. What is by contrast impermissible is to say that because demand for work in a particular art form is high, the state subsidy should be increased so that *avant-garde* work can be produced in that art form and "raise the popular taste" in a way state bureaucrats think it should be raised. There was plenty of evidence that this kind of thing happened as the new régime at the Arts Council got into its stride. Here for example is an account of just such an incident in one of the Arts Council's "priority" areas, dance, written by Nicholas Drogmoole in the *Sunday Telegraph* (11 November 1985):

> The dance world is still upset by the news that Robert North has had to give up as artistic director of Ballet Rambert.
>
> I understand that not so long ago the Arts Council representative on the Rambert board informed it that the Council's advisory committee was getting worried because Rambert was "too successful and too popular". Can this really be true? After all, you and I, as taxpayers, contribute to the Arts Council more or less willingly in the fond hope it will make the arts more accessible to wider audiences. Have they really this absurd élitist approach, that to be popular is somehow not art, which ought to be too incomprehensible and upsetting to do us any good?

Perhaps the Arts Council has a bureaucratic plan. It may think there is a minority audience for "difficult" *avant-garde* works, and its chosen role for Rambert is to meet that minority demand. So if it gets too popular and successful it has to be slapped on the wrist and recalled to the narrow path the bureaucrats have mapped out for it. If so, this is bureaucracy run mad. To stop artistic development being successful, just because it happens to contradict policy agreed in some official memo, is nothing but the dead hand of officialdom stifling the arts.

The authors of *The Glory of the Garden* received evidence from the Regional Arts Associations, some of it written on the assumption that the level of demand for, and the level of activity in, any art in any region, was directly proportional to the level of state subsidy it needed and received (not, as some might suppose, inversely proportional to it). They made much of apparent inequalities. Pleading for more money to subsidize drama in the region, Northern Arts gave as one of their reasons that "The Arts Council's direct contribution to drama here is lower than that to all but two other regions, both in terms of cash and per head of the population."[1] This kind of special pleading—to build the same kinds of arts buildings everywhere, ten miles from each other, and to have the same levels of state subsidy in all the same state-recognized arts—was encouraged by the Council, and it duly arrived in sackfuls. "Development" meant equalizing state aid, an equalization of subsidy which, it was assumed, would mean that the creation of "art" would somehow be evenly distributed, and access to it would be universal. Although dressed up in the management jargon of the eighties, the same kind of bureaucratic minds that masterminded the not very efficient wartime distribution of bacon seemed to be again at work.

Indeed the various proposals in *The Glory of the Garden* all seem to be more or less made with this "equalization" in mind. The intention, oft-stated, was not so much to maintain and encourage the best in art, as *to distribute art subsidy a bit more equally between London and the regions.* (A working paper from the Institute for Policy Studies had said that the Council's expenditure per head in Greater London was three-and-a-half times as much as that for the next-best-provided region, Merseyside.) But art and bacon are different things, and Liverpool is not London; so the Council's *Glory of the Garden* strategy, presented with such an air of hard-nosed facing of facts and such determined real-worldliness, soon acquired a faded air of bureaucratic fantasy, even of unwitting pathos.

The paper also, in spite of saying that it is quite impossible to devise any kind of formula for the apportionment of state subsidy between art

forms, concluded that the proportion of its funds spent on opera was too
high: "Thus the development programme...seeks to go some way
towards redressing the imbalance between spending on opera on the one
hand and spending on other music and dance on the other."

The conclusion was that the Arts Council was going to give "priority"
in its development programme to five main areas of work—Art, Dance,
Drama, Music—and Education! (There was relief that it had not chosen
to make Health, or Social Work, or the Defence of the Realm priorities,
at least this time.) New commitments in these five areas were to be
financed by the withdrawal of subsidy from ten music clients, ten build-
ing-based drama companies, five touring drama companies, six "training" centres, and—most importantly—by the winding down of the
"Housing the Arts" operation. As reading and writing were plainly of
less interest to the born again Council than the more politically rewarding
field of "Education", it also concluded that its spending on Literature,
never more than 1·5% of total expenditure, should be reduced by
some £350,000.

But overall, looking past the tough managerial platitudes to the actual
proposals—phasing out a revenue-funded client here and cutting funding
from a project there—the reader had a sense of mighty language hiding
midget action, and a suspicion that there was behind all this much-her-
alded flummery an unwritten political purpose. The new words "provision" and "development", left-overs from the post-war Ministry of
Housing, did not mean very much on the surface, but they were harbing-
ers of a new politicization of the Council. *The Glory of the Garden* was less
a strategy than a propaganda leaflet, renaming parts of the well-established Arts Council world, and dressing up the actions of the Council in
new "tough" language. At the time the brutalism of this new Arts
Council language was excused as "talking to the government in the only
language it understands", but it soon became apparent that the men at the
top of the restructured bureaucracy could think and express themselves in
no other way.

The pretence that the Arts Council was "in the business" of making
critical judgements was dropped. It was now in the business of "assessment". It "assessed" its clients according to a weird mixture of sociological, geographical, aesthetic, managerial, financial and educational
categories. There were the fourteen "criteria" published in *The Glory of
the Garden*, though not in any order of priority because, as the pamphlet
blithely announces, there *was* no order of priority:

> (a) quality of artistic product, including, as appropriate,
> standards of presentation, performance, design and direction, and
> their relationship to the company's overall programme;

(b)   actual and potential creative strength in relation to both new and established work;

(c)   the extent to which stated aims and objects are realized;

(d)   the fullest practicable use of facilities and the widest provision of the arts to the community;

(e)   education policy in relation to the artistic programme;

(f)   the employment and other opportunities extended to members of ethnic minority groups;

(g)   overall value for money, including any success in extending audiences through other media;

(h)   box office and attendance returns;

(i)   the company's success in raising local authority support and other income;

(j)   the efficiency shown in using available resources and the accuracy and control of budgeting

(k)   the urgency and nature of any fundamental financial problems;

(l)   the adequacy and security of tenure of premises;

(m)   the balance of provision between London and other regions;

(n)   the Council's existing declared policies, particularly the emphasis it places on full-time professional work.

The Council added the helpful rider that "Individual criteria may become of paramount importance in the assessment of any particular client"—without indicating how you could tell which of the fourteen standards would be applied to you.

If you were a client, you would be hindered, not helped, by this daunting list. You would know that the Council's declared policies ((n), above), had, since Lord Keynes's first broadcast, been confused and contradictory. You would also know that "efficiency" in the use of available resources during the production of a work of art ((j), above) is no kind of measure of excellence—would E. M. Forster have been a more efficient writer if he had written more words per minute? would Bacon be a more efficient painter if he spilt less paint on his studio floor? You would see, plainly enough, that these criteria are not criteria at all, merely an indication of some of the categories in which a public account may be given of decisions arrived at using other, secret, semi-articulated notions of what kind of arts organization was appropriate to the new Britain.

There is nothing about them—excepting the very first, nervously used word, which is got out of the way as quickly as possible—to suggest that we are here talking about the work of *artists*: composers, poets, novelists, choreographers, sculptors, *particular kinds of people*. The "criteria" could

be used to assess a departmental store, a prep school, a formation swim-
ming team, an airport shop, a hairdressing salon or fifty other kinds of
organization. Indeed there are many kinds of production line and many
kinds of retail unit that this suits better than it does the arts. There is
much about *The Glory of the Garden* which suggests that its authors might
have been happier looking into the national provision of, say, Chinese
restaurants, than they were looking into the "provision" of Art, Dance,
Drama or Music.

* * *

At all events *The Glory of the Garden* did make one group of people
very happy. It gave a lot of work to the fast-growing breed of "Arts
Consultants". They were now employed to advise arts organizations on
how to dress up their applications for state aid in the new jargon (Arts
Council officers advised their clients on which consultants they should
spend their subsidy on employing.) The game was to release the old state
arts subsidy under one of its exciting new names: "development" money
or "challenge grants", or "matching grant" allocations. Organizations
were encouraged now to go for "plural funding" (another gutsy new
term for the centuries-old practice of getting money from a number of
sources) but were encouraged to consult about which consultants could
best advise them about applications to each of the various schemes. This
meant that not only were there additional full-time bureaucrats in the
funding bodies and in each client organization,[2] but a swarm of consultants turgidly droned around the subsidized "arts world" writing reports
about applications and rewriting applications and writing responses to
applications—all in longwinded mimicry of the "real" boardroom
world.

The "strategy for a decade" not surprisingly had no very positive
effect upon the actual arts. In spite of the Council bizarrely giving "priority" to Education, eighties cutbacks in education budgets cut down
instrumental music teaching, some literature teaching, and many drama
activities in schools. The national network of Art Colleges (which had
produced many fine artists and incidentally many fine musicians, film-
makers, actors and writers too) was already in a desperate plight and did
not survive the decade. The book purchasing grants of libraries were cut,
and this meant that it was even less likely that new novelists could be
published, bought and read in sufficient numbers. Richer people spent
ever-larger parts of their disposable incomes on holidays abroad, and
proportionally less on supporting their local arts activities, which sadly
spent their time touting for domestic tourist support. The position of the
writer, artist and composer became steadily worse as the Arts Council

proudly announced that "the Arts" were "a great British success story".

The Arts Council, by adopting the government's language, had done nothing for artists but it had, for a while, saved itself. Occasionally, Sir William Rees-Mogg acknowledged that the Council's posturings bore little relation to real economics, real life or real art:

> I sympathize with the National Theatre, housed in that great concrete dreadnought on the South Bank, an expensive but unfortunately not a watertight ship. But I sympathize a lot more with the Everyman Theatre in Liverpool, on the edge of the worst area of social suffering and deprivation in England. The National Theatre gets £6.7m from the Arts Council; the Everyman, even after development, will get less than £250,000.

Thus Sir William a year after the publication of *The Glory of the Garden*. Apparently an admission of defeat. The Neighbourhood Cultural Watch, ever alert, had noticed an under-provision in Merseyside. Springing into action, the Arts Council had at once developed the organization. But, sadly, for the people of Liverpool it did not appear to make a ha'porth of difference.

Yet in the wider, political, sense victory had been achieved. *The Arts Council had been saved!* Sir William later assured Terry Coleman, in a *Guardian* interview, that Mrs Thatcher was very pleased with the way things had gone "in the arts". He meant, the way things had gone in the Arts Council—the way it had adopted the massively inappropriate language of the pre-war Business School to describe what British artists did, the way it discussed the arts as if they mattered only as economic counters, and the way it had discussed the life of art as if it were nothing more nor less than an *industry*. Heedless of all the warnings it had issued in its own youth against artists prostituting themselves by commercial activity, the wrinkled old Arts Council had, as it grew short of breath, struggled into a pair of gaudy commercial breeches, painted its eyes all-seeing and its nose hard, and cruised shamelessly forth to sell itself in the market place.

*   *   *

For those artists and critics who did not depend in any way upon the machinations of the Arts Council—fortunately, the majority—the eighties provided a richly comic spectacle. For those who did, and for the many who worked within the crumbling system, the decade was a tragedy. Promiscuously falling in with any kind of company, terrified (in Sir Kingsley Amis's excellent phrase) of being caught with its trousers up, the old body shuffled about the markets, endlessly pliable to the government's will, always ready to rat on an artist to comply with the latest managerial fashion, anything for a nod of acknowledgement and a bit of loose change from the government's purse.

The arts were now perceived of, assessed as, funded and discussed as an *industry*. "The truth," said Sir William Rees-Mogg magisterially, "is that the political economy of the arts is dependent upon the political economy of the nation." But for him the political economy of the arts and the arts were the same thing. "Art," he said in the same lecture,[3] "is simply one of the things crowded out by state over-expenditure, along with education, research, productive investment and other desirable goods." So the only art is state-subsidized art, and that art is a form of industrial goods, significant as a part of a state political economy.

The Arts Council language now took on an air intended to be business-like, but in practice brutal and boorish. Books, pictures, symphonies and plays became *products*, watchers, listeners and participants *consumers*, whose market habits were systematized by *arts marketers*, so that they could be gulled into purchases which fitted the planner's *market strategies*. Critics no longer searched for quality in art, but instead assessors looked for *managerial efficiency*, including the *minimizing of overheads*, and accurate *market targeting*. Assessors also carried out *audits of current management practices*, and examined arts organizations' *productive efficiency* and *sales potential*.

And the Arts Council's publications, now written in a kind of *Sun* newspaper rhetoric—everything asserted, nothing argued, nothing proved—hammered home the main claim that the arts' purpose was to increase urban wealth. They were not of course above tagging on every other virtue that they could think of, but making money for rich city developers was the dominant theme. Here, from a booklet called *An Urban Renaissance: the Role of the Arts in Urban Regeneration*, published by the Arts Council, is an altogether typical paragraph:

> The arts can make a substantial contribution to the longer-term revitalizing of depressed urban areas. Theatre, music and the visual arts—and the facilities for their enjoyment—are essential ingredients in the mix of cultural, environmental and recreational amenities which reinforces ecnomic growth and development. They attract tourism and the jobs it brings. More importantly, they can serve as the main catalyst for the wholesale regeneration of an area. They provide focal points for community pride and identity. Equally importantly, they make a contribution to bringing together communities which might otherwise be divided.

The pamphlet then devotes a short paragraph to "Regenerating Civic and

Individual Pride", a paragraph notable both for the fact that it comes close to being political propaganda for the Conservative Party, and for showing, as stagnation spirals downwards, that the new realists in the Arts Council had lost their forebears' abilities in using metaphor:

> The arts create a climate of optimism—the "can do" attitude essential to developing the "enterprise culture" this Government hopes to bring to deprived areas. Inner city stagnation is a downward spiral. Failure breeds failure, people lose confidence in their ability to succeed and consequently their will to try. The arts provide a means of breaking this spiral and helping people believe in themselves and their community again.

There is not much, it seems, that "the arts" cannot do. They reinforce economic growth, attract tourism, regenerate whole areas, bring broken communities together, give everybody confidence in themselves. (*That*'s what Lawrence did for Eastwood, and Donald Pleasance did for Worksop and Dylan Thomas did for Swansea.) And there's more yet:

> ·Arts facilities and other amenities act as magnets to attract other development and are useful marketing tools to show that an area is "up and coming".
>
> Businessmen in redevelopment areas already recognize the role of the arts as a catalyst for redevelopment.

So "the Arts" may not only be developed, but *re*developed. One must, with all humility, ask what other tools a modern government needs. The arts put the economy straight and attend to our psychological well-being. It would seem that the Arts Council should take over the reins of government.

Except, of course, that it is obviously all a sham, a ludicrous and shameful language game in which tired and rather desperate activities are described in exciting new political terms, and the decaying subsidized *corps* is described as if it is a Phoenix new risen. What could be more pathetic than Sir William Rees-Mogg, in the 1986–7 Arts Council Report, seeking to claim success for all this new "realism", pretending that until *The Glory of the Garden* had brought the arts world a smack of merchant enterprise all arts organizations had been state-dependent and unworldly?—

> Nevertheless the response of arts clients to the stringency of funding has been very enterprising. More and more arts companies have come to recognize that central government funding is only one of the sources from which their revenue will come.

Was all that terrible period of strategizing, confusion, redefinition and capitulation to "lucre's filthy charms" simply to persuade arts clients of what they already knew perfectly well—that the Arts Council was not their only source of funding? Why did nobody whisper to Sir William, before he wrought his dreadful havoc, that *they already knew*?

But Sir William habitually elevates platitudes to the level of Revealed Truths, and he goes blithely on:

> There is no doubt that the self confidence and success of those companies who have been able to do most for themselves is in direct contrast to the anxieties of those companies who are in proportionate terms most heavily dependent upon subsidy.

If that is true, then Council employees must have been terrified out of their wits. For the Arts Council is *wholly* dependent upon subsidy, and if its officers had been forced, like the employees of some of its client organizations, to find industrialists prepared to pay their wages out of their investors' profits, they would soon have been on the streets.

7

Dividing the Kingdom

Philistines and politicians have not in recent years seen the Arts Council of Great Britain as their enemy; indeed the new-style Council has taken to providing such people with lucrative employment. The Council's ruling junta seems latterly to have enjoyed basking in the praise of the building developers, financiers, industrialists and professional politicians whom it has set out to please. It has by contrast taken little account of the vociferous and varied criticism which has come increasingly during the past fifteen years from artists. Sometimes this has taken the form of resignations (from Roy Fuller in the mid-seventies to the entire Drama panel in the mid-eighties), sometimes of unwillingness to serve as artistic director of subsidized organizations, and sometimes of a direct critical attack. The best-known and most indefatigable embodiment of the latter school is Sir Kingsley Amis:

> My case... is not that arts subsidies from public money are unjust because they make the poor pay for the rich, true as that is, nor that they encourage waste in productions of opera and dramas (though they do) nor even that they inevitably attract "the idle, the dotty, the minimally talented, the self-promoters" as a distinguished poet put it when resigning from the Arts Council some years ago. I say that subsidy as such damages art... .[1]

In Amis's view, state subsidy (in the form of Arts Council grants) is nearly always fatal because the artist or arts organization is judged worthy of state aid by a *committee*, and is (fatally) *paid in advance*. Thus the public has no voice in "the arts" and the artist has no incentive to interest, engage or please the public. The artist's main incentive is to demonstrate that his or her work is *avant garde*. By way of demonstrating the danger this poses, Amis quotes Schoenberg, who started atonal composition in 1908: "I believe that a real composer writes for no other purpose than to please himself. Those who compose because they want to please others, and have audiences in mind, are not real artists."

Yet those whose utterances were of interest only to themselves, and who could not be understood by anyone else, were once not called "real artists" by most people, but were more probably thought to be mad. A composer was not considered to be a composer until audiences some-where listened to what had been composed and thought it music. If he sat day after day amusing himself by playing sounds which only he thought musical, we did not in former times send for a state music committee and urge that taxpayers' money be spent upon him, we sent for the physician. Nor were painters once thought to be worthy of state support simply *because* nobody liked what they painted. They became painters when (often after a struggle) enough people saw what they painted as pictures and thus paid attention to them. And (as Ian Robinson pointed out fifteen years ago, as something he "thought everybody knew") there is no such thing as a poet without readers.

The state subsidy system, however, bestows the title of composer, painter or poet upon those whom it subsidizes, and plainly some state arts bureaucrats do not think that the absence of listeners, watchers or readers seriously tarnishes their judgement. In the mid-seventies the Arts Council heavily subsidized a journal called the *New Review*, and in 1976 Robinson examined this curiosity in *The Times Higher Education Supplement*:

> The *New Review* could not exist without Arts Council subsidy, and it dawned on me that subsidy is replacing what I had taken to be a necessary condition for literature. A writer nowadays may look for readers, in the old-fashioned way—or alternatively he may do without readers and look instead for support out of the taxes.
>
> I pick on the *New Review* because it seems to have got the hang of the system better than older magazines still suffering, as from a hangover, from the wish to communicate and convince. For the *New Review* holds anything like a reading public in conscious contempt.
>
> For instance, one of its leading lights, the writer of pop lyrics and satirical verses Clive James, wrote a letter to *Private Eye* quite sublimely contemptuous of all judgement not subsidized by the Arts Council and not proceeding from his own clique. "As to the *New Review*'s contents, only people with a literary background are competent to judge."...Mr James's letter ended:

> > Charles Osborne (Literature Director of the Arts Council) is a man of wit, accomplishment and courage—an ideal appointee for the difficult job of backing a small number of worthwhile projects while being harried by a large number of mediocrities on behalf of an infinite number of fools. [30 May, 1975]

My comments are of course part of the harrying by mediocrities, but in all probability you, Dear Taxpayer, are one of the infinite number of fools. The equation is: mediocrities + fools = the reading public.[2]

With Amis, Robinson's argument is that the Arts Council system positively harms art, that what is paid for in advance is decided at best by a committee of well-meaning but secretive bureaucrats, or at worst by a clique, sensitive only to some prejudged notion of what is, according to their secret codes, "innovative", *avant-garde*, and new. The artist is thus not just relieved of any obligation to interest and please at least some of the general public, but is also encouraged to please the subsidizers by demonstrating that his work is "difficult", advanced, displeasing to the majority and therefore "in need" of public subsidy. (The bureaucrats will generally help things along by announcing that there is nevertheless a "need" and an unarticulated "demand" for this kind of baffling "art", and that it will, *once subsidized and "developed"*, attract business, improve inner cities, bring communities together, bring the tourists in, demonstrate a "can do" philosophy, and simultaneously soothe, stimulate and educate one and all.)

In recent years the dislocation of the state subsidy apparatus from the general public and hence from the real arts world has become more extreme. Recent Arts Council reports spelled out what its Music Department said in 1988–9 was "a strong feeling", that funding "should increasingly be used to support *innovation.*" Each decade has thus had its word for the action of keeping something going on state money simply because it suits the new bureaucracy. In the sixties, it was called "new" art; in the seventies the stuff came from Arts Council "initiatives"; in the eighties it was at first a sort of by-product of "development", and then, suddenly, it all depended upon a new process—described by a word from the "enterprise culture"—"innovation".

So what did the new cult word actually mean? Examination of the relevant glossy Arts Council pamphlets suggested that it had two meanings. In the first case *innovation* simply meant giving the old state subsidy to the well-established client organizations, *but under new, bureaucrat-friendly schemes.* That is, the Council described its old habits in bullish new eighties language. That kind of "innovation" was illustrated clearly enough by the figures showing that in 1987–8, three years after *The Glory of the Garden*, with its emphasis on devolution, new money, enterprise and change, the Arts Council was still spending 48% of its money in London, and more than half of that on the four jewels in its crown, the Royal Opera House, the Royal National Theatre, the Royal Shakespeare

Company, and the English National Opera Company. (Its own staff numbers in London had meanwhile risen to cope with devolution; in 1984–5 the Arts Council employed 161 people and in 1987–8 it employed 167.)

It was the second kind of "innovation" which was however more disturbing. For the Arts Council seemed, while producing piles of designer brochures puffing the mix of investment advice and town planning that they now called "innovation in the arts", to have more or less lost interest in flesh and blood artists and in the tangible things artists do. The Council seemed no longer even to be pretending an interest in real art or in real art's particular publics. It seemed to be interested only in the creation of wealth, in producing Public Relations brochures which put a gloss on sterile bureaucratic activities, and in the fierce political pledges that accompanied the "new realism" in fashionable London. So, as its interests were not so bound up with political and managerial style, it naturally became overwhelmingly interested in itself. In its own mind its own swelling bureaucracy seemed to have taken the place of art altogether. Indeed this new practice, "innovation", was ultimately a bureaucratic conceit, part-managerial, part-economic, part-political, and unrecognizably different both from the kind of things that the Arts Council was formed to do, and, in its first twenty years at least, from all that it did. Although, confusingly, the Arts Council still used some of the same tag phrases—still spoke of the "arms-length principle", of "peer-group assessment", of "centres of excellence" even—it now existed within a new and less human realm.

The 1986–7 Report—a model for any aspiring bureaucrat aiming to write high-sounding, meaningless business jargon—was the most striking example of this slide from the old Arts Council style, and indeed was an illustration of a pervasive bureaucratic vacuity which seemed at that time to permeate British officialdom. The Report had a strangely anaesthetized air, as if an inert computer intelligence had possessed the writers. It announced that the Council had created within its own bureaucracy a *Planning Department* with which the Arts Council could plan itself. This department, in its own first report to the nation, said that it had spent its first year experiencing its own existence. Meanwhile the *Literature Department* announced that the most exciting development of its year had been formulating a new policy. Not to be outdone, another bureaucracy called *"Combined Arts"* reported thrustingly that a new committee had been formed within its area "at the beginning of the financial year". The *Drama Department* said that the year's most significant event had been another enquiry into the state of the British theatre, under the chairmanship of Sir Kenneth Cork, while the *Touring Department*

alertly reported that it had reorganized its own office procedures.
The Report had a few, uneasy, references to "innovations" that were
not just rejigging of bureaucratic procedures, and which might have
seemed to be something to do with art. A closer look, however, suggested that these apparent lapses into cultural realms were no more to do
with art and the general public than the rest of the document. There was,
for instance, on page five, an account of an exciting innovation, apparently within the field of the Visual Arts:

> Following a unique feasibility study commissioned by the Arts
> Council, leading sculptors nationwide were invited to submit
> designs for a new landmark at Holbeck Triangle, Leeds, a piece of
> waste land leading into the City Station...a special large-scale
> work which will give train travellers a dramatic first impression of
> the city.

The paragraph is headed by a photograph of what looks like the thickly
whitewashed cadaver of an asexual yeti. The imagination plays upon its
likely impact on travellers pulling into Leeds City Station. The Report,
however, with a kind of preppy eagerness, explains why this kind of
"innovation" now counts, even at the planning stage, as fully fledged
Arts Council "art". The sculptor had been commissioned: "With back-
ing from the Arts Council, British Rail, Leeds City Council, and arts
groups in Yorkshire...." "Art" is thus blatantly defined as *any project
which has the right "funding mix"*. Likewise non-art is defined as anything
which actually exists, which some of the public like enough to pay for,
and which is not a part of the state "provision". The fact that Leeds City
Council eventually withdrew from the project, and *Whitewashed Yeti* was
never placed in its chosen wasteland, did not seemingly prevent this
bureaucratic "innovation" taking its place in the canon of the Nation's
"Art", part of the "great British success story".

With its own Planning Department monitoring every departmental
enquiry, each new allocation of responsibilities, each new internal assessment and all its internal reorganizations, the Arts Council seemed in the
1980s to set no bounds to its own fast-breeding bureaucracy. As outside
its well-guarded doors the reading public shrank, theatre attendances
overall dwindled, serious concert-goers diminished in number, dance
attendances took a downturn and arts centres trimmed their programmes, the Council announced that one of its greatest successes was its
Marketing Department. (This is another fascinating link that the Arts
Council "arts" have with the Milk Marketing Board, for since the
creation of that estimable body the consumption of milk in Britain has
steadily declined.[3])

Having sternly announced, at the time of *The Glory of the Garden*, that it had been spreading itself too widely and was going to concentrate upon the vital primary aspects of its work, the Council's actual attention wandered blearily across the ever-more-diffuse realms of managing, marketing and politics. Advertisements for (increasingly well-paid) posts at the Arts Council stressed that what was now required there was experience of management, business enterprise, skill in financial dealings, computer literacy &c. In smaller print the advertisements usually conceded that an interest in art would be a useful additional attribute, but no more than that. (In view of the Council's unthinking deference to businessmen, applicants were probably grateful that an interest in or knowledge of art did not disqualify them altogether.)

The Council's Art Directors no longer attended meetings of the Arts Council as of right—presumably so that the Minister's appointees from the "real world" should be free to discuss what really interested them—wealth creation, the development of the inner cities, the tourist trade, media franchises and so on—without being hampered by a lot of arty-farty irrelevances. So the talk in the Council's chambers sounded satisfyingly like that heard elsewhere in hard-nosed commercial circles, and the multiplying list of Arts Council panels, groups and projects committees now included the following:

Touring Board
Touring Projects Committee
Planning and Development Board
Education Committee
Training Committee
Monitoring Committee: Ethnic Minorities Arts
Monitoring Committee: Arts and Disability

—This in addition to fifteen other major committees and some standing committees including the *Policy and Finance Committee* and the *Enterprise Board*, which considered applicants under the Incentive Funding Scheme.

The Council had thus reached the point described by Michael Frayn in his satirical novel *The Tin Men* (1965) where the number of committees multiplies indefinitely, everybody is a member of every committee, and all committees are in continuous session. At that point the committee structure goes critical and (except for the committees endlessly producing reports for each other) no action can ever be taken. In similar fashion the Arts Council found itself in a state of high old managerial excitement, meeting followed meeting, paper followed paper, but it was quite unable even to take effective decisions about its own organization, still less address problems which Britain's parlous cultural state obviously posed.

The Council was by no means alone in its eighties madness. *The Times* added to its regular features a "Saleroom" column which described art works entirely in terms of their resale value. The B.B.C. first ensured the revitalizing of its commercial arm, B.B.C. Enterprises, and then re-arranged itself on proper business lines by appointing its senior accountant as Director General. The government's ministers, other neo-governmental agencies, and some local authorities, enthusiasti-cally joined in the same North Sea Bubble. Lord Gowrie resigned as Minister for the Arts, giving out that his minister's salary of £33,000 a year was insufficient to live on in London, and instead took a post as chairman of Sotheby's International (Art Dealers) at £150,000 a year. The Policy Studies Institute was paid by government to produce a 221-page document, *The Economic Importance of the Arts*, showing how good busi-nessmen were for the arts and how the arts could make businessmen even wealthier. And various cities and large towns, drawn in to this wealth-making hysteria, announced grotesquely expensive "redevelopment" projects, some of which were actually built.[4]

These strange edifices were doomed to be the tangible monuments of the political fantasies of the eighties—raw vistas of parking lots, shopping arcades, hotels, theme parks and a few art-and-craft corners, all built on expensively borrowed money, all with their developers featured in the same way in the same newspaper supplements, all trying to entice the same tourists by the same marketing devices, all paying the same consul-tants, and all doomed to become a burden on local community-charge payers, with multiplying debt-service charges and rocketing staffing costs. After forty years, here at last were the People's Pleasure Pal-aces!—but palaces in which spending was the highest pleasure, and consumption the only satisfaction; palaces which were monuments to the twin gods of enterprise and wealth-creation—half-finished, half-let and half-used.

*   *   *

In old age, dementia takes many forms. Some elderly people gently return to the days of their youth, and the ancient body houses youthful memories and gentle child-like fantasies. But some seem to be more totally possessed, and live their waking lives haunted by terrible unreal-izable obsessions. In its dotage the Arts Council of Great Britain sadly fell prey to both mental infirmities, and, though humoured by its friends, seemed finally to pass beyond the compass of rational minds.

In 1988 it was announced that Peter Palumbo, a rich developer, would be Lord Rees-Mogg's successor as Chairman of the Arts Council. Some immediately cast him as state executioner, sent in to perform the happy despatch of an ailing quango. But it was the Minister, Richard Luce—who announced upon his appointment as Minister that he knew nothing about the arts (meaning, it turned out, only that he had not at that time had his card marked by the metropolitan arts establishment)—who finally decided that the kindest thing was to divide up the kingdom and to put the Arts Council in a position from which it could do little further harm to its clients and to itself. He took the first steps in December 1988, telling the House of Commons that he had asked the retiring Head of the Office of Arts and Libraries, Mr Richard Wilding, to review state funding of the arts in Britain:

> The review will be primarily concerned with the structure of support, and the way in which the various parts of the system fit together. It will be conducted on the basis that the arm's length principle will continue to govern the allocation of money within a given total and the making of artistic judgements, and that a substantial amount of decision-making should continue to take place at the regional level.

The last point was emphasized by Luce in his published letter (8 December 1988) to Lord Rees-Mogg. He announced that no change was intended in the way the Arts Council awarded grants to the four London jewels in its crown, but stressed again the importance of *regional* decision-taking—in other words, he signalled that he intended to diminish the central Arts Council's role, and to enhance that of the Regional Arts Associations. Wilding began work on his review in January, 1989, and it was published in September of that year.

Meanwhile, a second and potentially more explosive report on the state arts subsidy system was being assembled. The National Audit Office's review of the Office of Arts and Libraries and the Arts Council[5] was presented to the Commons Public Accounts Committee on 14 May 1990, but its contents were known to the Minister well before then. It was—like the Wilding Report published six months previously—highly critical both of the overlapping bureaucracies of the subsidized arts world, and of the Arts Council's London bias which, in spite of the Council's repeated protestations that it was not a body that believed London was always best, had actually *increased* during the eighties. In 1984–5 London spending was 5·5 times as much as the average regional spending. By 1987–8 it was 6·3 times greater.

Wilding's Report foresaw a greatly increased role in the state support system for the Regional Arts Associations, which he suggested should be re-named Regional Arts Development Boards. The Arts Council should have far fewer grant-aided clients, should trim its staff drastically and should become a kind of federal meeting house in a streamlined new system. A suggestion in the Report, that some of the twelve R.A.A.s should merge, producing fewer and larger Regional Arts Development Boards, ran into much opposition. A suggestion that officers of the same art form in national and regional funding bodies should come together to form "colleges" (art colleges, music colleges and so on) was largely ignored.

When it came to announcing his decisions, Luce went rather further than Wilding had suggested and further than most people had expected. He severely trimmed the Arts Council's responsibility for direct funding, and set up systems by which many of its direct grant-aiding powers *would* be transferred to the new enhanced Regional Boards. He foresaw the Council in future playing a "more strategic role". Its new chairman, Peter Palumbo, immediately and strangely defined this strategic role as planning "for the millennium". There was not, he said, a moment to lose! More oddly still he suggested shortly afterwards that the Arts Council might find a part of its new role in looking after Britain's cathedrals. . . .

The Secretary General of the Council, Luke Rittner, who made no secret of his distrust of Luce's plans, and of his lack of sympathy with the new Chairman, resigned his office. Peter Palumbo meanwhile redecorated his, at his own expense, and adopted the same management style that others—Alan Bond in Sydney, Donald Trump in New York—had made the hallmark of the new-style big-league all-purpose cultural developer. He undertook triumphal tours of the regions, announcing innovation, with development here and enterprise there. And quite quickly Palumbo's Arts Council seemed to spin away into its own demented world. It was announced that each year at least one major British city was to be culturally *developed*. By the year 2000 the country would be dotted with spruced-up arts venues (all ten miles from each other, and exactly the same. . .). And there would be a new age of arts patronage by those sensitive souls the eighties had made rich. . . .

But, in its delirium, the Arts Council seemed also to take delight in hearing once more the catechisms of its childhood. As soon as he had announced its radically diminished role, Luce reassuringly said, as if to humour a subject with obviously fading faculties, that the Arts Council's role would "not be diminished", and then further announced that, in spite of his direct intervention to relocate the state funding agencies for the arts, the "arm's length principle", which protected the Arts Council against exactly that kind of interference by elected politicians, remained inviolate. Spokesmen for the Council seemed to find some comfort in these soothing words.

Meanwhile Palumbo launched a billion-pound appeal to get the fabric of the country's cultural and heritage buildings—whatever they may be—"in the best condition" by the year 2000. And, in the lee of this swashbuckling developer's talk, the aged Council produced a handbook, *The Arts Council Guide to Building for the Arts*. It included the glad tidings that the Council was to rename state aid once more: money would now be given out for arts buildings under a *Capital Incentive Scheme*. It also included a Foreword by Mr Palumbo, in which he gave the Developer's keen viewpoint on arts buildings:

> Well-designed theatres, concert halls and exhibition spaces, and buildings which are sensitively converted, enhance our experience for the arts—the design, acoustics, lighting and the way that a space is used within a building to present a performance or objects affect our perception of what we see or hear.

"Companies," the Report says elsewhere, "have been floundering for years not knowing what to do about the growing needs of their buildings." With analysis of this depth and precision now on offer, it was clear that companies could stop floundering. Instead they could give way to despair, that an Arts Council that was supposed to be speaking for art could no longer think or write coherently, and was now so deluded that it believed buildings had needs, more significant than the needs of artists.

And, at the last, the Council fell into total delirium. In November, 1990, the Government gave a final bribe to the Council—with a new title, an "enhancement fund". The "arts world" assumed that this was to allow the dying Council to pay off its moral creditors by rewarding those companies that had got themselves into artistic trouble through following its commercial guidelines. Instead, the Council announced from its deathbed that it would financially enhance those companies that had done the opposite and had accumulated the most impressive deficits. Thus the Royal Shakespeare Company, which had accumulated a £3,000,000 deficit, was given a 30% increase in its grant allocation. By contrast, the South Bank Board, which had loyally followed the Arts Council's commercial directives, had produced a "business plan" and wiped out a £1,000,000 deficit in two years (at some cost, be it said, to the arts programmes produced there), was given a lower-than-inflation increase of 5·5%.

The Royal Opera House, at constant odds with the Council, and with a mountainous deficit, was rewarded with a huge increase. The Welsh National Opera, much more compliant, was given such a tiny one that it feared it may follow Kent Opera into oblivion. As *The Times* said (19 December, 1990), in a remarkably severe editorial, "All the sophisms the

Arts Council employs to dress up its decisions cannot disguise the fact that, once again, those that moaned the loudest have been most richly rewarded. Metropolitan push has once again triumphed at the expense of the regions." The latest Secretary General of the Council testily explained to the savage hordes in early December that you must expect this kind of thing when you had an Arts Council that took decisions solely on the grounds of artistic excellence, as of course the Arts Council of Great Britain, in its firm and unflinching way, invariably did. A month later he said, with equal fervour, and somewhat more convincingly (*apropos* an emergency meeting about saving the Welsh National Opera) that the Arts Council actually relied upon its political cunning and its financial ingenuity, and not upon boring old principles at all. It could change its mind about anything at any time it liked and, in a word, would take any old decision providing that it got the Council out of trouble,

Meanwhile the deposed Prime Minister had in her retirement honours list made Peter Palumbo a life peer, for services to the arts (making him, rather memorably, P of the Arts Council). The celebrations were muted in Tyneside, where the Northern Stage Company faced a 20% cut in grant, and somewhat less than wholehearted in Bristol and Liverpool, where the repertory companies faced standstill grants. (It was pointed out that the inflated salaries of the senior Arts Council bureaucrats would, if put to that less destructive purpose, easily bale out those companies.) Everywhere, the press bemoaned the Council's contradictions, its crazed self-righteousness, its inability to see artists' needs, its arrogance towards the provinces and its pusillanimous crawling to London's power-brokers. *The Times* ended its editorial with a memorable call for the Arts Council to be summarily despatched:

> Confusion is now total and the momentum behind Richard Luce's devolution strategy has disappeared. Reform of arts subsidy is urgently needed. [This] sorry display of arts corporatism should make Mr Palumbo's council a prime candidate for the chop, in favour of a revitalized arts ministry. If the new arts minister, Timothy Renton, quails, his paymasters at the Treasury should wield the knife for him.

In Memoriam

So the Arts Council of Great Britain shuffles towards its final rest:

> Last scene of all
> That ends this strange eventful history,
> Is second childishness, and mere oblivion,
> Sans teeth, sans eyes, sans taste, sans everything.

It has at the end lost interest in art and artists, excepting their use in "cultural diplomacy", their use in trade, their use as tourist attractions, or in urban wealth creation. So it will not move the Arts Council's guardians much to point out that none of their *arts strategies*, *prescriptive planning*, *new realism*, hard-nosed *assessments* and general adoption of the seamier jargon of the *enterprise culture* has in the last twenty years produced one undeniable work of art. Nor will it be thought a telling objection to "the great British success story" if I say that the *new realism* has nowhere increased audiences and readerships for the arts. But it *has* increased bureaucracy everywhere. As at a theatrical performance nowadays where bureaucrats and technicians invariably outnumber the actors, so in the British subsidized "arts" the bureaucrats outnumber the artists.

The "great British success story" of the Arts Council has been a bureaucratic success. The "increases" have been in the realms of officialdom—in the spawning of "Development Officers", or the interbreeding of arts consultants—rather than in numbers of playwrights, painters, or readers or viewers. "Policies" have nothing directly to do now with the nurturing of artists, their readerships and audiences, but with the promulgation, through the usual bureaucratic means, of new functions to which the state arts bureaucracy may itself be put. Adoption of the fashionable bureaucratic processes—a politically correct "funding mix", adoption of an appropriate range of "policies" on the issues of the day, setting of "key objectives" and constant self-examination through enquiry and report—is what has marked out a successful organization in the eyes of the latter-day Council. And this coagulate of bureaucracy is really what the Arts Council has meant by "the arts". When it speaks of "the arts" this is all that it now sees. Not great music, great paintings, great drama, all bright and distinct, but instead a blurred and tacky mass of marketing and management and money and politics.

So we must cry, with Cornwall,

> Out, vile jelly!
> Where is thy lustre now?

And we must look with fresh eyes upon the real arts, and see them individually and sharply once more. The Arts Council should be closed down immediately, and with it must go its terrible language. We could then see, clearly enough, that in the sense the Arts Council used the term, there never was such a thing as "the arts". There never was one undifferentiated glob called "art", that consisted of state-aided organizations and state bureaucratic procedures, which attracted tourists, rebuilt inner cities, brought communities together, cured unemployment and regenerated civic pride (but still somehow required an annual government handout). That notion of "the arts" was generated by the Arts Council which had to define a product to justify its own existence, and it must be expelled from public usage immediately. We must ensure that the fledgling Regional Arts Boards, the Local Authorities and the Foundations that will, upon the death of the Arts Council, now have more to do, do not inherit the diseased legacy continued use of that term would bring.

Nothing the Arts Council has done that will not be better done when it is disbanded. The major state performing companies—the jewels in the old Arts Council's crown—will be directly grant-aided by government, as the national galleries and museums already are. The Regional Arts Boards will be free to develop, as they should, in their different ways, responding to local artists and local interests rather than to national strategies worked out by a metropolitan mafia.

Their main difficulty will be in ridding themselves of the effects of the Arts Council's language. It will not be easy for those who have been touched by the mania—who have perhaps even "testified" to the success of some funding scheme, urban enterprise or bureaucratic development—to see things straight once more. Difficult to remember that there is no such thing as "the arts", no single "crisis in the arts", and no simple economic effect of "the arts". There are, however, novels and plays, poems and pictures, dances and symphonies, songs and operas, all distinct, some in need of patronage, some not, but all with different needs, in different realms—needs that cannot be met by forcing them to fit the same bureaucratic machine.

For every step that an arts funding organization takes towards making itself a more efficient bureaucratic entity—creating its own planning unit, setting itself three-year "objectives", streamlining its line management—is a step away from its real purpose. For managerial practices in such an organization cannot exist prior to the creation of the art the organization exists to serve, and prior to the judgements it must bring to that art. Prescriptive planning, by which "priorities" in the arts are determined before a word has been written or a note composed, invites artists to respond to a bureaucratic plan.

Yet an important rule for a funding agency is that bureaucratic procedures must be created to suit what artists do; it is the bureaucracy that must respond to art. The second rule is that a funding organization must above all else keep itself alert to recognize what is good. That means that a good arts funding organization will be in a constant state of creative flux, measuring its success by the liveliness of the artists and art, not by the achievement of business objectives set years before.

And that will mean that its accountability—and so much of the damage the Arts Council has inflicted upon the arts has been done to pious cries of "accountability"—will be surer and more convincing. The Arts Council distorted the processes of critical judgement (that which it was set apart from government and commerce to do, because those processes *are* different from making political or commercial judgements). It did so out of funk. It recruited amateur politicians and businessmen and commercial high flyers on to its boards and panels because it had no real faith in the arts, and sought to legitimize itself in the eyes of merchants of enterprise. As the processes of seeking out genuine talent, or making critical judgements, were beyond its new heroes, the Arts Council cravenly made its processes, its managerial systems, and its language, of a kind commercial minds felt easy with. And that meant that it accounted for itself to government in the government's own political and commercial terms. That pleased some politicians, but it also meant that there was no further need for an arts council that acted in that way.

So Richard Luce delivered his thrust, and soon another Minister will deliver the *coup de grace*. Though the Council will continue, even on its death bed, to protest that its destruction means the destruction of the arts, in truth each of the arts will be liberated from a bureaucratic stranglehold. The Council will also insist that its end means an end to the government funding of the arts, but that is not true either. Removal of the Arts Council would remove one layer in the cumbersome process of grant aiding, and could give another £5·5m a year to artists rather than to bureaucrats. Nor will it mean the end of the arm's length principle, for the organizations newly funded direct from government will have the same independence of action as the managements of the national museums and galleries have enjoyed for a century and more, and the Regional Development

Boards will have the same relationship to government as the central Arts Council once had.

The Arts Council cannot be buried without acknowledging that, most particularly in its youth, its officers achieved some good things. Even in its dotage it can be said that whatever the results of their actions at least its members bore no ill-intent towards the arts—one remembers Raymond Williams sadly shaking his head and saying of his fellow members of the Council "All such well-meaning people, but so wrong"—and their actions will not have been wholly unproductive if we all learn the obvious lesson from the experience. It is not enough to say that critical judgements about the arts must be made at arm's length from politicians. It is not enough to say that they must be made within one special kind of organization. They must be made, not by developers and kings of commerce, but by people who understand the arts as well as they understand the arts business—that is, they must be made by alert, courageous and lively critical minds, wherever they may be found.

Appendix A

i

THE ARTS COUNCIL
ITS POLICY AND HOPES

By Lord Keynes

Reprinted from " The Listener" of 12 July, 1945

In the early days of the war, when all sources of comfort to our spirits were at a low ebb, there came into existence, with the aid of the Pilgrim Trust, a body officially styled the "Council for the Encouragement of Music and the Arts", but commonly known from its initial letters as C.E.M.A. It was the task of C.E.M.A. to carry music, drama and pictures to places which otherwise would be cut off from all contact with the masterpieces of happier days and times: to air-raid shelters, to wartime hostels, to factories, to mining villages. E.N.S.A. was charged with the entertainment of the Services; the British Council kept contact with other countries overseas; the duty of C.E.M.A. was to maintain the opportunities of artistic performance for the hard-pressed and often exiled civilians.

With experience our ambitions and our scope increased. I should explain that whilst C.E.M.A. was started by private aid, the time soon came when it was sponsored by the Board of Education, and entirely supported by a Treasury grant. We were never given much money, but by care and good housekeeping we made it go a long way. At the start our aim was to replace what war had taken away; but we soon found that we were providing what had never existed even in peace time. That is why one of the last acts of the Coalition Government was to decide that C.E.M.A., with a new name and wider opportunities, should be continued into time of peace. Henceforward we are to be a permanent body, independent in constitution, free from red tape, but financed by the Treasury and ultimately responsible to Parliament, which will have to be satisfied with what we are doing when from time to time it votes us money. If we behave foolishly any Member of Parliament will be able to question the Chancellor of the Exchequer and ask why. Our name is to be the Arts Council of Great Britain. I hope you will call us the Arts Council for short, and not try to turn our initials into a false, invented word. We have carefully selected initials which we hope are unpronounceable.

I do not believe it is yet realized what an important thing has happened. State patronage of the arts has crept in. It has happened in a very English, informal, unostentatious way—half baked if you like. A semi-independent body is provided with modest funds to stimulate, comfort and support any societies or bodies brought together on private or local initiative which are striving with serious purpose and a reasonable prospect of success to present for public enjoyment the arts of drama, music and painting.

At last the public exchequer has recognized the support and encouragement of the civilizing arts of life as a part of their duty. But we do not intend to socialize this side of social endeavour. Whatever views may be held by the lately warring parties, whom you have been hearing every evening at this hour, about socializing industry, everyone, I fancy, recognizes that the work of the artist in all its aspects is, of its nature, individual and free, undisciplined, unregimented, uncontrolled. The artist walks where the breath of the spirit blows him. He cannot be told his direction; he does not know it himself. But he leads the rest of us into fresh pastures, and teaches us to love and to enjoy what we often begin by rejecting, enlarging our sensibility and purifying our instincts. The task of an official body is not to teach or censor, but to give courage, confidence and opportunity. Artists depend on the world they live in and the spirit of the age. There is no reason to suppose that less native genius is born into the world in the ages empty of achievement than in those brief periods when nearly all we most value has been brought to birth. New work will spring up more abundantly in unexpected quarters and unforeseen shapes when there is a universal opportunity for contact with traditional and contemporary arts in their noblest forms.

But do not think of the Arts Council as a schoolmaster. Your enjoyment will be our first aim. We have but little money to spill, and it will be you yourselves who will by your patronage decide in the long run what you get. In so far as we instruct, it is a new game we are teaching you to play—and to watch. Our war-time experience has led us already to one clear discovery: the unsatisfied demand and the enormous public for serious and fine entertainment. This certainly did not exist a few years ago. I do not believe that it is merely a war-time phenomenon. I fancy that the B.B.C. has played a big part, the predominant part, in creating this public demand, by bringing to everybody in the country the possibility of learning these new games which only the few used to play, and by forming new tastes and habits and thus enlarging the desires of the listener and his capacity for enjoyment. I am told that to-day when a good symphony concert is broadcast as many as five million people may listen to it. Their ears become trained. With what anticipation many of them look forward if a chance comes their way to hear a living orchestra and to experience the enhanced excitement and concentration of attention and emotion, which flows from being one of a great audience all moved together by the surge and glory of an orchestra in being, beating in on the sensibilities of every organ of the body and of the apprehension. The result is that half the world is being taught to approach with a livelier appetite the living performer and the work of the artist as it comes from his own hand and body, with the added subtlety of actual flesh and blood.

I believe that the work of the B.B.C. and the Arts Council can react backwards and forwards on one another to the great advantage of both. It is the purpose of the Arts Council to feed these newly-aroused and widely-diffused desires. But for success we shall have to solve what will be our biggest problem, the shortage—in most parts of Britain the complete absence—of adequate and suitable buildings. There never were many theatres in this country or any concert-halls or galleries worth counting. Of the few we once had, first the cinema took a heavy toll and then the blitz; and anyway the really suitable building for a largish audience which the modern engineer can construct had never been there. The greater number even of large towns, let alone the smaller centres, are absolutely bare of the necessary bricks and mortar. And our national situation to-day is very unfavourable for a quick solution. Houses for householders have to come first.

And so they should. Yet I plead for a certain moderation from our controller and a few crumbs of mortar. The rebuilding of the community and of our common life must proceed in due proportion between one thing and another. We must not limit our provision too exclusively to shelter and comfort to cover us when we are asleep and allow us no convenient place of congregation and enjoyment when we are awake. I hope that a reasonable allotment of resources will be set aside each year for the repair and erection of the buildings we shall need. I hear that in Russia theatres and concert-halls are given a very high priority in building.

And let such buildings be widely spread throughout the country. We of the Arts Council are greatly concerned to decentralize and disperse the dramatic and musical and artistic life of the country, to build up provincial centres and to promote corporate life in these matters in every town and county. It is not our intention to act on our own where we can avoid it. We want to collaborate with local authorities and to encourage local institutions and societies and local enterprise to take the lead. We already have regional offices in Birmingham, Cambridge, Manchester, Nottingham, Bristol, Leeds, Newcastle-upon-Tyne, Cardiff and Edinburgh. For Scotland and for Wales special committees have been established. In Glasgow, in particular, the work of the Citizens Theatre is a perfect model of what we should like to see established everywhere, with their own playwrights, their own company and an ever-growing and more appreciative local public. We have great hopes of our new Welsh Committee and of the stimulus it will give to the special genius of the Welsh people. Certainly in every blitzed town in this country one hopes that the local authority will make provision for a central group of buildings for drama and music and art. There could be no better memorial of a war to save the freedom of the spirit of the individual. We look forward to the time when the theatre and the concert-hall and the gallery will be a living element in everyone's upbringing, and regular attendance at the theatre and at concerts a part of organized education. The return of the B.B.C. to regional programmes may play a great part in reawakening local life and interest in all these matters. How satisfactory it would be if different parts of this country would again walk their several ways as they once did and learn to develop something different from their neighbours and characteristic of themselves. Nothing can be more damaging than the excessive prestige of metropolitan standards and fashions. Let every part of Merry England be merry in its own way. Death to Hollywood.

But it is also our business to make London a great artistic metropolis, a place to visit and to wonder at. For this purpose London to-day is half a ruin. With the loss of the Queen's Hall there is no proper place for concerts. The Royal Opera House at Covent Garden has been diverted to other purposes throughout the war. The Crystal Palace has been burnt to the ground. We hope that Covent Garden will be re-opened early next year as the home of opera and ballet. The London County Council has already allotted a site for a National Theatre. The Arts Council has joined with the Trustees of the Crystal Palace in the preparation of plans to make that once again a great People's Palace.

No one can yet say where the tides of the times will carry our new-found ship. The purpose of the Arts Council of Great Britain is to create an environment, to breed a spirit, to cultivate an opinion, to offer a stimulus to such purpose that the artist and the public can each sustain and live on the other in that union which has occasionally existed in the past at the great ages of a communal civilized life.

ii

The Secretary General's Report

Arts Council of Great Britain 1989–90

It is sometimes difficult to know exactly how to start the Secretary-General's report. One thinks of major events of the year under review. One thinks of themes, the major innovations, and tries to pick an opening that somehow catches the atmosphere, the character of the year just ended. On this occasion I have to say there is no difficulty whatsoever in deciding how to begin.

My opening has to be taken from the final paragraph of my preface to the Council's last annual report. In that closing paragraph I warned that all the benefits of three-year funding could be blown away by an unexpected or significant rise in inflation. I hoped that government would heed that warning. Well, one year on, the Council finds itself struggling to help a rising tide of client organisations facing financial difficulties as a direct result, not of mismanagement or bad box office, or lack of entrepreneurial skills, but simply because inflation has outstripped grant-in-aid by 6%.

The strains are being felt throughout the arts world, and although none of us wants to return to the days of the permanent whinge about lack of funds, it seems to me that a failure by government to recognise this situation will be a cruel slap in the face to an arts world that has done so much to adapt to the market economy of the 1980s. I believe the Minister for the Arts has sympathy for this predicament and I hope he will be able to persuade his colleagues in the Treasury of the true nature of the problem and that they in turn will respond by increasing their commitment, as would any investor in a successful business that was facing a temporary difficulty.

The year being reviewed was a year that saw the Council under two microscopes. The National Audit Office began its review in August 1988, and this will not be completed before the end of 1989, so its findings and repercussions must necessarily await our next annual report. Suffice it to say, we take this review extremely seriously, and while resisting the temptation to be over-confident, I do believe the Council is an efficient and effective organisation as a result of the many changes that we have introduced in the last five years and we therefore await the findings of the review reasonably sure that we will not be found wanting in our adherence to our key objectives or the way in which we achieve them.

In January of this year Richard Wilding embarked on his review, commissioned by the Minister, of the English arts funding structure and to examine the working relationship between the Arts Council and the Regional Arts Associations. Again, we await the results of this review at the time of going to press. The relationship between the Council and the RAAs has always been spiced with a creative tension verging on rivalry. If the Wilding review results in a new structure that brings greater unity to the two existing systems of funding whilst preserving the essential qualities of local decision making and national overview, then the future will be an exciting one.

The introduction of three-year funding has resulted in the publication of our first Three-Year Plan. This document clearly shows the Council's objectives for the next three years and how we can measure the extent to which those objectives have or have not been achieved. As a public body distributing taxpayers' money it seems to me this is an important step in opening up the Council to wider public scrutiny and accountability.

Change in leadership of any organisation is always important. On March 31st 1989 Lord Rees-Mogg retired after seven years as Chairman of the Council. He had served longer than any previous Chairman, with the exceptions of Lord Clark and Lord Goodman. Peter Palumbo has paid eloquent tribute to his predecessor in his own introduction to this report. Lord Rees-Mogg steered the Council through a turbulent and sometimes hostile sea. His period of office saw the Council having to do its job with limited resources; it faced the challenge of abolition of the Metropolitan Authorities, the introduction of the infamous Clause 28, the welcome amendments to copyright law, three-year funding, *The Glory of the Garden* policy review. Turbulent and challenging times indeed. I believe the Council owes Lord Rees-Mogg a great debt of gratitude.

In the first 12 months of the Incentive Funding scheme, almost £4.5m was allocated in awards. Those who received awards project a total increase of more than £13m in their *annual* self-generated income by the end of 1991. Forty-eight arts groups from all over Britain have been successful in their bids for incentive funds. Successful applications are based on sound three-year plans—something from which all organisations stand to benefit. Planning does, and should, involve a lot of hard work. But we have been careful to ask only for information which organisations should have readily available, and for plans which should be of real benefit to applicants whether or not they receive an award. This year we have simplified both the guidelines and the application process, to rebut any lingering criticism that the scheme is unnecessarily complex and bureaucratic. And the Council has approved an extension to the scheme which is designed to provide training and other help to arts organisations at an early stage in the planning process.

An incentive award is a stimulus for private sector contribution to the arts, and the scheme as a whole is an agent for encouraging the arts world towards better management practices and greater self-reliance. More and more arts groups are testifying to the scheme's success.

The Council is frequently criticised for giving grants that someone felt should not have been given; sometimes for not giving a grant, or more often, for not giving enough. We are sometimes criticised by artists, sometimes by politicians, occasionally by an aggrieved taxpayer. All this is as it should be. If the Arts Council did not cause a little controversy then I do not think we would be doing our job properly. It does, however, put an added pressure on the staff and I want to pay tribute to the dedication and professionalism of a staff that has reduced in size from over 300 in 1983 to 175 in 1989. They have responded magnificently to the challenges of the eighties, adapting with speed and enthusiasm to new policies, new objectives and new work practices. They are passionately committed to the arts that they serve and I am proud of them and grateful to them for what they do.

Of course, it is the artists and the performers who make the artistic life of our country, but just as every performance or exhibition needs technicians, designers and many others behind the scenes, so the distribution of subsidy needs its backroom team. The team at the Council is constantly striving to get the best for the arts by giving the best of itself.

Rapid change is taking place in all walks of life and the arts and the Arts Council are not immune. As this report goes to press we await the outcome of those two potentially important reviews and of our request to the Government to acknowledge the difficulties caused by the rise in inflation. All three could result in major changes. We shall welcome any changes that lead to a better deal for the arts. We shall not welcome change for change's sake. We shall defend to the hilt that which has been built up over 40 years of funding by an institution, the Arts Council, working entirely at arm's length from the governments that have funded it.

Luke Rittner

*   *   *

from the Chairman's Report

There is one further factor to which neither government nor the private sector have given sufficient thought, and it is high time that they did: the advent of the new millennium that is now less than 11 years hence. In one sense you may say it is no more, no less than another moment in time. In another, however, an event of profound symbolic significance and one, incidentally, that none of the five billion people inhabiting this planet will ever see again. I regard it as some great national marker towards which we should be directing collectively all our efforts and attention so that when the second hand ticks past midnight into the 21st century our house is in order, socially, economically, culturally and in terms of world stability. If we are able to achieve that sort of order it will be the happiest of endings as well as the happiest of beginnings for generations yet to come.

Peter Palumbo

Appendix B

SECRETARY GENERALS OF THE ARTS COUNCIL

with their dates in office and previous employment

Mary Glasgow 1946–1950
Secretary, Council for the Encouragement
of Music and the Arts

Sir W. E. Williams 1950–1963
Director of the Army Bureau of Current Affairs
and Director of the Institute of Adult Education

N. J. Abercrombie 1963–1968
Senior Civil Servant, Admiralty and Foreign Office

Sir Hugh Willatt 1968–1975
Solicitor, Nottingham

Sir Roy Shaw 1975–1983
Professor of Adult Education, University of Keele

Luke Rittner 1983–1990
Director of the Association for Business Sponsorship
in the Arts, Bath

Anthony Everitt 1990–
Deputy Secretary General, Arts Council of Great Britain

Notes and References

CHAPTER 1

1 Keynes's broadcast is an appendix to this book.

2 The Committee, later the Council, for the Encouragement of Music and the Arts.

3 The phrase is one of those quaintly put into new words by successive arts reports. In the 1965 White Paper, noting "increased demand" for the arts throughout Britain, it airily said of the regions that "each can have something that is supreme in some particular field."

4 The scale of arts activity in pre-war Britain has been consistently belittled by the post-war Arts Council. It is interesting to look at some figures. There were for example 530 museums in Britain in 1928, and by 1938 more than 650 museums and galleries. The *Statistical Review* of 1938 suggests that between 1933 and 1938 artists in Britain earned on average £2·5m in commissions from industry, and the last pre-war census of 1931 gave a figure of 10,000 visual artists working in Britain, considerably more than in recent accounts.

There were more than 120 major touring theatres in Britain in the thirties, 650 other theatres, and more than forty repertory theatres. After the Second World War, before subsidy became widespread, there were about 400 commercial weekly repertory companies in Britain. (See R. A. Jerrams, *Weekly Rep*, Peter Andrew Publishing Co., 1991.) The B.B.C., in addition to rescuing the Proms, had in 1930 created Britain's first full-time symphony orchestra. In 1932 Beecham established the London Philharmonic, and by 1935 Britain had twenty-four professional orchestras. In addition to the Old Vic and Covent Garden, and the work of the D'Oyly Carte, opera was served first by the British National Opera Company, then by the Carl Rosa and four other smaller touring companies.

5 Keynes assumes all artists are male. That may be a reason for thinking that in the same way fishermen call their vessels "she", the state vessel of the arts might be female, a school*mistress*. One cannot help thinking, irreverently, how perfectly the late Arthur Marshall would have played the role.

6 Nothing is new. As a result of a suggestion made in Sir Walter Besant's *All Sorts and Conditions of Men*, Britain already had a People's Palace. It was situated in the Mile End Road, seated 2,500, and had a magnificent organ. It was opened by Queen Victoria in 1887 and was funded by Mr Barber Beaumont and the Drapers' Company.

7 W. E. Williams's article appeared in *Picture Post*, 2 January 1943, in an edition especially assembled by Julian Huxley.

8 The Entertainment National Services Association was not at arm's length from anything. It produced and managed all its own shows directly.

9 Lady Clark is the wife of Sir Kenneth Clark. There is no evidence

that they (unlike Keynes) had more than the customary number of fingers, but every evidence that they stuck those they had into a great many pies.

10 Kenneth Clark, *The Other Half: a Self-Portrait*, 1977, p. 27.

11 See "Keynes, Lawrence and Cambridge" in F. R. Leavis, *The Common Pursuit*, 1952.

CHAPTER 2

1 R. Harrod, *The Life of John Maynard Keynes*, New York, 1951, p. 401.

2 *The Listener*, 12 July 1945.

3 Williams in the Sir William Williams Memorial Lecture, given in 1981 to an invited Arts Council audience.

4 B.B.C. research suggests that in the years immediately after the war one third of the entire adult population listened to *Saturday Night Theatre*, and rather more than that, some 40%, listened to light music programmes such as *Henry Hall's Guest Night*.

5 *The First Ten Years*, 11th Arts Council of Great Britain Report, 1955–6, p. 6.

6 The additional money for the Festival of Britain was paid to the Arts Council in 1951–52, increasing their annual grant from £675,000 in 1950–51 to £875,000. The following year—before we accepted the "fact" of inflation—it fell back to £675,000.

7 The fullest and funniest account of the controversy is in A. P. Herbert's *No Fine on Fun* (1957)—one of the few books written about arts administration which would be well worth reprinting.

8 Clark, *The Other Half*, p. 129.

9 Williams was the inevitable appointment because the only other candidate in the traps, John Reith, was assumed by the capital's king-makers to be barking mad.

10 C. Landstone, *Off-Stage*, 1953, pp. 192–3.

CHAPTER 3

1 Similarities with Mussolini's pre-war state come again to mind. "Cars of Thespis" took state opera, drama and music, stages on temporary state constructions, to every town and village of Fascist Italy.

2 Arts Council Annual Report, 1969–70. I fear that Lord Goodman's wickedness has not yet permitted him the leisure in which to write. I offered him the opportunity of contributing to a book of essays, *The State and the Arts*, which I edited in 1980. Contributing would have involved no taint of avarice, as the fee was, in Lord Goodman's own word, "derisory". Nevertheless, he refused.

3 Published in Britain by Penguin in 1989; p. 110

CHAPTER 4

1 "Arts Laboratories" were places, like Frankenstein's cellar, where unusual, unnatural and unwanted entities could be stitched together by obsessed artists. Some lasted five years and one—Birmingham's—lasted much longer than that. In spite of appearing to meet the necessary criteria—tiny audiences,

big state grants, incomprehensible art products—they are now no more than a historical footnote. Odd, as they were eminently defensible on arts bureaucrats' grounds.

2 The Finance Officer of the Arts Council was once rung by someone from the Treasury who said that it was possible the Arts Council could have a "little bit more" money. "But," the official added, "I need an argument. Is there anything you can suggest?" "The price of wood has risen," said the resourceful officer. "You need a lot of wood for scenery and suchlike." "Excellent!" said the Treasury man.

Thus are government arts policies determined.

3 The word *community* is now used in the "arts world" simply as a warm buzzing noise. It was not always thus. In the early days, following Geoffrey Whitworth's work in the twenties and thirties, it was used in the arts in its American sense of "amateur, neighbourhood activities". By the sixties, however, "community arts" only existed when paid government bureaucrats ran otherwise amateur activities.

4 The Arts Council is of course not the largest employer of artists in Britain. Local government, advertising and broadcasting all give more to the arts.

CHAPTER 5

1 Charles Osborne, *Giving It Away: the Memoirs of an Uncivil Servant*, 1986.

2 The Arts Council publication *Organisation and Procedures: Report of the Working Party*, 1979. The similarities with MI5 are particularly strong at this period. A senior Arts Council officer was asked to meet a government official, to discuss the Arts Council grant, in St James's Park, and to his astonishment found himself walking up and down the pathways talking *sotto voce* with a man in a neutral macintosh. Panels on occasion got on their hands and knees and searched the Arts Council's premises for bugs, and when it was decided to extend Sir Roy Shaw's contract, before the Conservatives took office, the Council moved to a "safe house" (the headquarters of London Transport) to talk.

3 In the late seventies administration itself did not become tougher. It just hid its swelling bureaucratic belly in a corset of tough managerial language. A 1980 survey by the Consumer Council noticed a marked increase both in bureaucracy and in the application of bureaucratic language to non-bureaucratic problems.

4 Baumol and Bowen, *Performing Arts: the Economic Dilemma*, New York, 1966.

5 H. Baumol and W. J. Baumol, "The Future of the Theatre and the Cost Disease of the Arts", in *Bach and the Box*, Akron, 1985.

6 *Private Eye* called Roy Shaw (as he then was) an "obscure provincial academic". This was unfair, as Shaw did not aspire to the status of an academic. Hearing that the Gulbenkian Foundation was to give modest support to an independent academic "Think Tank" in the arts, Shaw wrote to the Foundation's Director demanding that this "unre-

presentative body" be immediately disbanded.

7 The research on inflation in the arts "proved" nothing so simple. Costs do not increase ahead of inflation, even in the orchestras which usually seem to be the target for economic studies in "the arts", simply because orchestras are "labour-intensive". Indeed, at an early stage in this research project Shoesmith and Millner pointed out (Akron, 1982) that if promotions and engagements for the four London orchestras were aggregated, three out of the four of them showed, between 1967–8 and 1979–80, a *decrease* in (average) real costs per performance!

8 It is perhaps noteworthy here that the present author has never been rejected, indeed has never applied for, an Arts Council grant. Likewise he has never applied, nor been rejected, for an Arts Council post. It follows from Sir Roy Shaw's categorization that, since I criticize that Arts Council, I must therefore be a Philistine.

9 Roy Shaw did once hold a public debate—at the Hayward in 1977—to permit his Arts Council officers to explain themselves. (A TV journalist had attacked the selection of paintings.) The Visual Arts Director, however, maintained the long tradition of having nothing to do with the public by sitting through the entire debate without saying a word.

10 Members of the Arts Council are appointed, and their appointments terminated, by the Minister. Dr Richard Hoggart had his appointment discontinued during Shaw's time because, Shaw was told, he was disliked "at Number Ten".

CHAPTER 6

1 *Getting Our Act Together: a Review of Drama Provision in the Northern Arts Region*, 1983.

2 A "Development Officer" was asked in the author's hearing to say what the job entailed. "It is my job to persuade the local authorities to appoint development officers." And then? "To write reports." And then? "The reports usually recommend further appointments." Of what? "Well... ."

3 W. Rees-Mogg, *The Political Economy of Art*, an Arts Council lecture given at IBM South Bank London, 11 March, 1985.

CHAPTER 7

1 Kingsley Amis, "Setting the Arts Free", in *The Art of the State*, Adam Smith Institute Papers, 1989.

2 Ian Robinson, in *The Times Higher Education Supplement*, 12 March, 1976.

3 The link between the subsidized arts and the Milk Marketing Board became closer in 1989 when the boss of the Milk Marketing Board was made Director of the Barbican Arts Centre. The next announcement was that in 1990 the Royal Shakespeare Company would withdraw for four months from the Barbican.

4 But, happily, some "development projects" cause a local outcry, and aren't allowed to proceed. Lawrence's Eastwood is threatened by a "Town Centre Development" with superstores, tourist centres, mass car parks and so on. The local protest group have banners which

say, quoting Lawrence, "The Country Of My Heart", adding, "Don't Let It Be Broken".

5 *OAL: Review of the Arts Council of Great Britain*, National Audit Office, House of Commons Paper 382, 1990.